GREECE
The MONOCLE Handbook

MONOCLE

First published in the United Kingdom in 2025
by MONOCLE and Thames & Hudson Ltd,
181a High Holborn, London, WC1V 7QX
thamesandhudson.com

First published in the United States of America in 2025
by MONOCLE and Thames & Hudson Inc,
500 Fifth Avenue, New York, New York, 10110
thamesandhudsonusa.com

MONOCLE is a trading name of Winkontent Limited

British Library Cataloguing-in-Publication Data
A catalogue record for this book is available from
The British Library
Library of Congress Control Number: 2024945740
For more information, please visit *monocle.com*

MIX
Paper | Supporting
responsible forestry
FSC® C013123

This book was printed on paper certified
according to the standards of the FSC®

Edited by *Chiara Rimella*
Introduction by *Andrew Tuck*

Designed by MONOCLE
Proofreading by MONOCLE
Typeset in *Plantin*

Printed in Italy by *Graphicom*
isbn 978-0-500-96631-0

Cover images
Front cover (from left)
Corfu by Andrea Pugiotto; Church by Marco Arguello;
Mehoti Kindelis, Crete by Marco Arguello
Back cover (clockwise from top left)
Corfu by Andrea Pugiotti; The Rooster, Antiparos by
Marco Arguello; Maison Bardot by Yiorgos Kaplanidis;
Select, Ioannina by Marco Arguello

Greece

The MONOCLE Handbook

DISCOVER GREECE
PART 01

We travelled the length and breadth of the mainland and traversed sun-soaked archipelagos to scope out the best this fabled European nation has to offer. Visit traditional tavernas and thoroughly modern restaurants; designers, shoemakers and ceramicists reinterpreting Greece's ancient crafts; and the best places to recline along the glittering Athenian Riviera and around the storied islands, where clear blue skies and seas mark some of the country's coveted destinations. *Kaló taksídi!*

PUT DOWN ROOTS

PART 02

Fallen in love with Greece? Perhaps it's time to extend your stay – maybe indefinitely. In this chapter we show you the best places to open a business, introduce you to the architects and designers who can help turn your dream into a reality and peek inside some Greek homes along the way. We also hear from bold entrepreneurs who have already made the move.

ADDRESS BOOK

PART 03

Use this handy guide to help you plan your next trip. Here we present a full list of our favourite places to stay, eat, shop and visit organised by region. Whether you're heading to Thessaloniki or Santorini, we've got you covered.

Whether you're just visiting for a sunny weekend getaway or planning to stay for longer, *Greece: The Monocle Handbook* makes the perfect travel companion. What are you waiting for?

INTRODUCTION

ANDREW TUCK
Editor in chief

There's one thing you must be careful of when visiting Greece – it will seduce you. Unsuspecting travellers arrive by ferry on a sunny isle, or book a table at an Athens restaurant, then when they are back home, it seems that all they can think is: "How do I get back there?"

Perhaps they'll try recreating some of the dishes they tasted on the harbourfront that night or uncorking a delicious bottle of assyrtiko white wine, but without the summer heat, the white houses or the colours of the bougainvillea dialled up to a 10, it's just not the same. So, a year later, they find themselves returning not just to Greece, but to the island, the restaurant, that somehow already feels like it's their spot.

In some ways, Greece is a small nation, with some 10.5 million inhabitants, but broken up into so many islands, two glorious and very different main cities, and with a mainland that takes in everything from craggy mountains to fertile plains, it would take you a lifetime to cover all of it. Even Greeks seem awed by the vast number of places that deserve attention. Hence this Handbook.

In the fourth outing for this series (hopefully Portugal, Spain and France are already on your bookshelves), we guide you around the nation with the help of Greek friends, writers, architects and designers. We show you where to visit and introduce you to Greek entrepreneurs and makers keen to articulate a deeper story about their country. And, of course, we recommend tavernas, hotels and retail outposts where we think you will get closer to the soul of Greece.

What makes the Handbooks special is that they also cater to people who are totally seduced by their encounter with Greece. People who think, "Could I put down roots here?" That's why, in the coming pages, we will introduce you to folk who have made that leap – and flourished – and even recommend a place or two for you to take up residence.

So, what are you waiting for? Welcome to *Greece: The Monocle Handbook*. But don't say we didn't warn you.

MAPS

The borders of the modern Greek state were a slow work in progress since its independence from the Ottoman Empire in 1830. The Dodecanese – a group of islands in the southeast Aegean – was the last area to unite with the rest of the country in 1947, after the Second World War.

Greece is a peninsula at the tip of the Balkans in the Mediterranean Sea, that borders Albania, North Macedonia, Bulgaria and Turkey. Despite its relatively small size, Greece boasts the second-longest coastline in Europe. The Ionian and Aegean seas are dotted with around 6,000 islands, but only around 200 are inhabited. More than three quarters of the mainland is covered by mountains – of which the most significant is the Pindus range – and countless steep, tumbling gorges. Greece's diverse landscape contains thousands of plant varieties, with a significant amount endemic only to the country. Made up of 13 regions, its peaks delineated areas, allowing for cultures and cuisines to develop independently between them. There is also the autonomous ancient monastic community of Mount Athos in the north, where only men can visit. Mountainous terrain is interspersed with fertile plains in central and northeast Greece, while the rest of the country is made up of its sun-drenched islands. Every archipelago – from the Ionian to the Dodecanese – has a distinct character and architecture.

Cyclades
Whitewashed cubic houses with colourful doors, stunning beaches and rugged terrain.

Ionian Islands
Lush hills sliding into turquoise waters and towns with Italian influences.

Crete
Greece's largest island is the southernmost point of Europe.

Attica
Home to the sprawling capital, Athens, which is surrounded by the mountains and sea and site of the Acropolis.

Peloponnese
Picturesque villages, beautiful beaches and exclusive resorts. An easy travel destination from Athens.

Northern Greece
Bordering the Balkans, its verdant and craggy regions include Vikos gorge, one of the world's deepest.

CYCLADES

DODECANESE

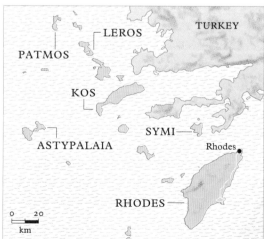

NEED TO KNOW

▬▬▬▬▬▬▬▬▬

We turn a spotlight on the nation's traditions and quirks, from the way its people enjoy their food (enthusiastically, with as many friends as possible), to lessons in relaxation and the enigmatic ways of Greek grandmothers.

EATING CULTURE
More the merrier

As an extension of Greece's eminently relaxed lifestyle, restaurants that open for lunch continue to serve meals until closing time. Usually, locals muster for lunch between 14.00 and 15.00 and you'll be pressed to find anyone eating out before 21.00 to 22.00 in the evening. Eating and drinking alfresco is unfailingly an option, irrespective of the weather, with most venues equipped with heaters. Dinners are usually a highly social affair, bringing families and friends together, so expect a lengthy and loud process. A variety of dishes strewn across the table are meant to be shared, so ordering food tends to be democratic. The bill isn't, however – it can be split, but Greeks prefer to take turns in footing it. At the end of the meal, a plate or two of complimentary fruits or desserts will be served.

RELAX
There's no hurry

Blame it on the heat, philosophy or good food, but Greeks take it easy. Shops don't necessarily open on the dot, sipping a coffee takes a while and partying goes on through the night. With the sun around for the best part of the year, this casual approach manifests itself in the dress code too. Don't worry about trousers and buttoning up for dinner, though sunglasses are considered *de rigueur*. Ladies will look out of place in heels strolling through the cobbled streets of villages and the islands. Smoking in restaurants and bars is prohibited, but don't be surprised if anyone lights up a cigarette after hours.

PATRON SAINTS
What's in a name?

Greeks have a wonderful way of celebrating their loved ones without having to remind the subject of growing older. Name days are celebrated with gifts and cards. Giorgos, Eleni, Kostas and Yiannis are among the most popular names, while the country shuts down on 15 August when Panayiotis, Panayiota and (the virgin) Maria are honoured. Some name days change because of Easter celebrations, and even names that aren't in the Christian Orthodox calendar enjoy their special moment: All Saints day.

YIAYIA(DES)
Grandma knows best

Once the sun sets, you'll frequently bump into *yiayiades* (grandmothers) sitting outside homes, often on traditional patchwork rugs placed on the elevated edge of pavements. At the end of a day of errands and once the temperatures have dropped, it's time for them to cool off with knitting, coffee and talking over the "news" of the day or contemplating – and discussing – passers-by. It's *veggera* time: a custom still seen on islands, in villages and in some urban neighborhoods. The *yiayiades* always enquire on the origins of unfamiliar faces and will enthusiastically talk to you – even if you don't understand a word.

LANGUAGE
Ancient wisdom

"It's all Greek to me" has more meanings than one. As one of the oldest languages in the world, you'll find many English words have roots in Greek. A mathematical, logical and allegorical language, it combines words to create new ones: *kalokairi* (*kalo*, good and *kairos*, weather) means summer, while *anoixi* (from the verb *anoigo*, to open) is spring. The closest-sounding European language to it is Castilian Spanish – not only because of its passionate intonation (which makes friends often sound like they're arguing, even if they're having a perfectly amicable conversation) but also because of similar sounds like th, ps and k. Some words intrinsic to Greek nature are untranslatable, like *kefi* (good mood and vibes) or *philotimo* (friend of honour). *Ya* is an easy, shortened word useful for greeting, used for both hello and goodbye. Adding -mas (*yiamas*) turns it into a useful shortened version of cheers when clinking glasses, and means "to our health". Try not to confuse *nai*, which is "yes" but nearly sounds like no, and *ochi*, which resembles okay, but means "no". You'll hear Greeks address their close ones as *malaka* a lot, but it's actually a curse word, so only use it with friends. *Opa* can be used like oops but is also an enthusiastic exclamation to underscore excitement for anything from food to dancing.

DRINKS
Liquid sunshine

Greece's grape-based drinks industry has been undergoing a renaissance in the past decades. Its bottled wines are starting to stand out in the international scene despite winemaking being around for millenia. And yet, grapes don't only produce fine wine. The pomaces distilled into *tsipouro*, *tsikoudia*, *raki* or *souma* are widely enjoyed throughout the country before, with or after a meal. Their cousin, ouzo, comes from mixing grapes with aromatic herbs, particularly anise. All these potent drinks are sipped (not gulped) ice-cold, with ice or diluted in water. For a digestif, depending on where your Greek travels take you, you'll find some exclusively local liqueurs. *Mastiha* spirit is processed from the mastic tree grown on the island of Chios. Look for cinnamony *tentura* in and around Patra, tangy *kitro* in Naxos and sweet kumquat liqueurs in Corfu.

FERRIES
Joining the dots

With all inhabited islands serviced, ferries are the nation's preferred way of travelling. Barring strikes and bad weather, schedules tend to be punctual. But the summer months come accompanied by strong *meltemi* winds that even seafaring Greeks can't tame and which sometimes put a halt to departing journeys. Moreover, while the days of the crisis are gone, the people still enjoy a good protest to make their discontent heard, so make sure to check ahead for disruptions before planning your trip.

PART 01

DISCOVER GREECE

Take a tour of the country's best hospitality,
design, culture and architecture – plus the beaches
and outdoor spaces not to be missed.

Whether you want to lounge on the beach, be revitalised by the
mountain air or do some urban exploring, Greece has a setting to suit
you and a hotel to match. Here are our top choices.

WHERE TO STAY

Hospitality is at the thriving heart of the Greek economy. Its inns and hotels cater for every type of stay: from laid-back and rural to high-end and secluded. Whether you're dreaming of waking up to the sight of the Aegean or staying within the ancient walls of a historic town, our selection of hotels will deliver a blend of traditional charm and modern luxury. No matter where you choose, there will always be rich history, good food and breathtaking landscapes. While the islands are dotted with whitewashed villas, sugar-cube-styled boutique hotels and cabins hidden in the cliffs, the mainland offers options from serene retreats nestled in olive groves across the Peloponnese to stone manors set in the Epirus forest. In Athens, restored neoclassical mansions have been joined by a new generation of casual boutique hotels in up-and-coming neighbourhoods. Everywhere, Greece's signature warm approach to hospitality will inevitably make you feel at home.

THE EDIT

1 **Coastal hotels**
From polished upscale outposts to whitewashed island guesthouses, Greece has sea-lapped hotels to match its long and wildly varied coastline.

2 **Rural hotels**
Properties from ancient to modern that are immersed in Greece's fertile landscape.

3 **Urban hotels**
Grand dames and fresh-faced establishments from which to explore Greece's cities.

4 **The experts**
Three hospitality insiders give us their thoughts on the present and future of the country's hotel industry.

COASTAL HOTEL
THE ROOSTER
Antiparos

Situated in the remote northwest of the Cycladic island of Antiparos, The Rooster is the Platonic ideal of a stripped-back, serene beach hotel. "Antiparos is all about calm and that's what we're trying to achieve," says owner Athanasia Comninos. "We want to keep our footprint to a minimum." Hidden around the 30-acre estate, in between sand dunes and gardens, 16 contemporary villas made from island stone blend into the surrounding landscape. Designed by Athens-based architects Vois, each room also incorporates influences from Comninos' travels to Brazil, Mexico and beyond.
theroosterantiparos.com

Much to crow about
The Rooster's simplicity belies its innumerable offerings: there's alfresco feasts and starry suppers of traditional Greek cooking at the outdoor restaurant and bar, as well as a tranquil spa for facials, deep-tissue massages and treatments. The team can also organise fishing trips with local sailors or a scuba dive in the blue waters of the Aegean.

COASTAL HOTEL
NIKOLAOU RESIDENCE
Aegina

The island of Aegina in the Saronic gulf gained its creative reputation from the many artists who lived there in the 20th century. For a glimpse of the life of one of its most famous former residents, painter Nikos Nikolaou, you can now stay at his home, which has been turned into six guesthouses: the work of his nephew, Athens-based architect Theodore Zoumboulakis (*pictured*). "Nikolaou taught at the Athens School of Fine Arts but lived here all year, commuting to and from Piraeus," says Zoumboulakis of his uncle. After inheriting the property in 2001, the family wanted to open it to visitors but running it just as a museum would have been financially challenging. Combining it with a guesthouse allowed them to keep it accessible and also viable. "We have so many childhood memories of this place and it was always on our minds to breathe life back into it," Zoumboulakis says. Filled with canvasses, sculptures and the artist's book collection, this treasure trove of a space is itself a pretty portrait of what the artists saw in Aegina. *nikolaouresidence.gr*

COASTAL HOTEL
MÈLISSES
Andros

Sitting at the end of a dirt road, a 20-minute drive from the island's port, Mèlisses (Greek for "bees") is almost silent except for the swash of the sea and the occasional bleating of goats. Expect honey-coloured sunsets that can be admired from the terrace while sipping on a sundowner to the hum of the waves. Its owner, Allegra Pomilio, calls herself a "host" and can often be seen catering to her guests' whims with a smile. When the hotel – also her home – opened to guests in 2018, it did so as a culinary project and a venue for retreats and small-scale events. Today, the food and cooking classes are still fundamental to proceedings. Born in Italy, Pomilio spent her summers sailing around Greece with her aunt and uncle. Having later moved to France to work with a cookery author, she now peppers Mediterranean influences into her activities. Fresh, native vegetables grow mere metres from the family-style table where guests enjoy and share the fruits (and vegetables) of their culinary lessons.
melissesandros.com

COASTAL HOTEL
AMMOS
Chania, Crete

A short drive from the bustling historic town of Chania, Ammos represents a crisp, modernist take on the white-walled Greek tradition, overlooking the bigger of two sandy coves. Mornings are slow, starting with a dip in the pool or a walk along the beach. Evenings follow much the same recipe, with the rooftop bar basking in rosy light at dusk. "We wanted a calm space people could escape to," says owner Nikos Tsepetis (*pictured*). "You can meditate there, do yoga in the mornings or enjoy a drink watching the sunset." Choose from views overlooking either the garden or the sea. *ammoshotel.com*

Ammos bouche
"We offer simple, uncomplicated Greek cuisine," says Tsepetis. "It's healthy and easy – just the kind of food you want to eat when on holiday here." Choose from a meze spread, spicy prawns with feta, a Cretan *kalitsounakia* (cheese pie) and other freshly made treats.

COASTAL HOTEL
BRATSERA
Hydra

Named after the vessels on which Hydra's sponge fishers sailed across the Mediterranean to North Africa in the 1860s, the Bratsera Hotel occupies the building where sponges were processed. A thoughtful renovation saw the defunct factory become a charming hotel – which opened in 1992 – without forgetting its maritime roots. Former owner Christina Nevrou asked friend and architect Dimitris Papacharalampous, who studied restoration with Unesco, to oversee the two-year transformation. Papacharalampous dutifully preserved the building's 18th-century features: the original antique tiles have been painstakingly reconstructed, the house's dark wooden beams exposed and the door to each of the 25 rooms constructed from old shipping containers that once carried cargo on the bratseras. "I didn't want to just create another minimalist Greek hotel," says Papacharalampous, who later took over ownership. "Hydra is a protected island with a rich maritime heritage and Bratsera offers a tangible insight into that." *bratserahotel.com*

COASTAL HOTEL
GUNDARI
Folegandros

Gundari sits atop a cliff in the southern end of the Cycladic isle of Folegandros. Echoing the island's wild, rocky landscape, Gundari's interiors feature earthy browns and limestone chosen by Australian owner Ricardo Larriera. The 25 suites and two villas are designed by Athens-based architects Block722. All have windows framing the Aegean, but some include subterranean rooms with infinity pools and dark wood joinery in shaded, cave-like spaces sheltered from the summer *meltemi* winds. Chef Lefteris Lazarou brings city flair from his Michelin-starred Athens kitchen and one of the city's best bars, Line, helps with cocktails. *gundari.com*

COASTAL HOTEL
MEDITERRANEO
Kastellorizo

"It's really a balcony onto Turkey," says Marie Rivalant, a French-born architect who owns the Mediterraneo hotel on Kastellorizo, in the easternmost corner of the Dodecanese. With pale blue columns and an ochre façade reflecting in the waters beyond, the hotel's design choices were shaped by Rivalant's heritage but also display Anatolian accents. Guests enter the 18th-century building through a garden of oleander and red geraniums, while the seven guest rooms are decorated with paintwork in breezy blues and minty greens. Greek icons hang from the walls and wood-panelled beds are offset by Turkish kilims and antique furniture. On the breakfast terrace, you'll be served pastries, eggs, yoghurt and fruit on a long trestle table. "Guests meet here, spend time together, then become regulars and come for two or three weeks," says Rivalant with a grin. Activities organised by the hotel suit the slower rhythm of life: there's yoga (hosted by Rivalent herself) or boat rides to secret swim spots.
mediterraneokastellorizo.com

COASTAL HOTEL
DEXAMENES
Kourouta, Peloponnese

COASTAL HOTEL
ARCHONTIKO ANGELOU
Leros

Just a short stroll from Leros's Alinda Beach, Archontiko Angelou is a hidden gem. This listed house dating from 1895 contains nine rooms and suites, and was originally built for owner Marianna Angelou's grandparents. Every sweetly old-fashioned room is decorated individually and furnished with antiques. The exterior spaces are equally charming; a quiet flower garden sweeps around the building, overlooked by shady terraces. Here, delicious organic, homemade breakfasts are served in the shade of ancient trees, containing vegetarian and gluten-free delicacies. Now and then, Archontiko Angelou has also hosted retreats and weddings.
hotel-angelou-leros.com

Growing up in a Peloponnesian village, Nikos Karaflos became fixated on a derelict 100-year-old winery near Kourouta beach and fantasised about converting it into a hotel. When his family acquired the estate in 2003, his childhood ambitions began to take shape. Being an engineer himself, with a stint at acclaimed architecture firm K-Studio (*see page 187*) under his belt, Karaflos knew he wanted to enlist his former colleagues to create a minimal, clean-lined structure mostly using steel, glass and timber. "The challenge was not only to preserve the history of the buildings, but also to bring them back to life," says Karaflos. "I had a strong vision to leave the walls almost untouched. K-Studio was aligned but also upgraded the idea." There are 34 "Wine Tank" suites on offer – a series of industrial-looking rooms dotted around the property. For something more traditional, you can opt for the two "Chem Lab" suites: larger, more spacious rooms right on the seafront, where Karaflos first imagined his dream hotel.
dexamenes.com

COASTAL HOTEL
BELVEDERE
Mykonos

New generation
The Belvedere was previously known as the Villa Stoupa and had been hosting famous artists, intellectuals and international celebrities since the early 1920s. It reopened as the Belvedere in 1995 and the Ioannidis siblings took over management of the hotel from their parents two years later.

With theatrical curved forms and minimalist decor by architect Domna Ioannidis and NY-based Rockwell Group, the Belvedere opened in 1995. "It's a space where socialising comes naturally," says owner Nikolas Ioannidis, who runs the hotel with his siblings. Natural materials like marble, stone and wood reflect the surrounding landscape; the hotel's 43 rooms and suites all have open-plan layouts and large windows to bring in natural light and Aegean views. Every detail, down to the narrow pathways between buildings and the rooms' low balconies, fosters a sense of community.
belvederehotel.com

COASTAL HOTEL
THE WILD
Mykonos

Contrary to what its name may suggest, the Wild in Mykonos is a haven of relaxation. Its name is actually inspired by the brave fishermen who used to go to sea from this former fishing village. The hotel leans into Mykonos's more unassuming, natural side: founders Alex and Philip Varveris brought years of expertise working for their father's design studio Moda Bagno/Interni Group into this project, which opened its doors in 2019. The 40 rooms and suites were designed using soft leather and linen fabrics, handcrafted lampshades and antique decorative objects. Each suite has a private pool, but it's also worth trying the spa's hydrotherapy waterfall cave.
thewildhotel.com

COASTAL HOTEL
PARILIO
Paros

Kalia and Antonis Eliopoulos, the owners of Parilio, have a knack for marrying minimalist Cycladic architecture with modern design. In 2018, when the pair bought this hotel in the northwest of Paros between the rock formations of Kolymbithres and the harbour town of Naoussa, there was no luxury accommodation on the island. The experienced hoteliers – who also run three hotels on Santorini – converted the existing bungalows and with Interior Design Laboratorium from Athens created 33 suites, some with their own pool, roof terrace or private jacuzzi. For the interiors, the designers chose warm, earthy colours and natural materials as a backdrop for statement ceramics by Marrakech-based studio LRNCE. A cross-shaped pool is the centrepiece of the hotel: Michelin-starred chef Thanos Feskos serves his island cuisine just beside it at his Paron restaurant. The grilled fish of the day in a saffron hollandaise emulsion with glazed vegetables is a particular highlight.
pariliohotelparos.com

COASTAL HOTEL
PAGOSTAS
Patmos

Hidden on a cobbled street in the Patmos town of Chora, this three-room guesthouse is a peaceful bolthole. "Our focus was on paring everything back rather than adding anything," says Gregoris Kambouroglou. He leased the property in 2021 with wife Maria Lemos – also behind Athens' Mouki Mou store (*see page 91*). Craftsfolk from around Greece made bespoke pieces for the hotel with the help of designer Leda Athanasopoulou, while the garden was created by landscape architect Helli Pangalou, allowing the couple to put a minimalist, upmarket spin on the idea of a Greek home. *pagostas.com*

Holy spirit
Patmos is known as one of the holiest locations in the country, so it is fitting that Pagostas is next to a convent. "The name comes from the abbot who built this complex in 1597," says Kambouroglou. The convent was added in 1607.

COASTAL HOTEL
LASPI
Pefkali, Peloponnese

Athens-born artist Alexandros Ntouras spent his summers along this stretch of the northern Peloponnese coastline as a child. It's here he opened a duo of guesthouses named Laspi in 2022. "I had the idea to start a hospitality project that combines architecture, design and art," he says. Young Athenian architecture studio Askiseis Edafous was tasked with creating the two properties as its first-ever commission. The design involved slotting together vast slabs of raw concrete in a brutalism-inspired construction that juts precipitously from the hillside. Ntouras worked on the interiors himself: his design carefully balances the concrete walls with warm, wooden surfaces, diaphanous curtains and plenty of greenery. The villas, named Petres ("Stones") and Skóni ("Dust"), accommodate six guests each and are available for rent year-round. During the summer, each house has a private pool on the ground floor or – if guests are feeling adventurous – they can amble down to the rocky coastline below.
laspi.life

ISTORIA
Santorini

Among Santorini's glittering destinations, Istoria stands out for its originality. Overlooking the black sands of Perivolos, the hotel rethinks the "more is more" idea of luxury undertaken elsewhere on the island. Athenian architects Interior Design Laboratorium were asked to transform this formerly dilapidated residence and rather than demolish it, the team revived the building while preserving as much as possible. The result opened in 2018 and feels more farmhouse than hotel, but retains the hallmarks of a high-end property: private pools, individual terraces, handmade furniture and a courtyard restaurant by executive chef Yiannis Kioroglou. *istoriahotel.gr*

COASTAL HOTEL
VERINA ASTRA
Sifnos

While its sister property, Verina Terra, sits on the beach of Platys Gialos, Verina Astra's suites and rooms, built out of Sifnian stone, cling to the cliff to the east of the island, which makes them feel closer to the expanse of the sky than the blue-and-white Panagia Poulati monastery below. In the day, the breeze blows through their bohemian interiors. On-site restaurant Bostani (which means orchard) serves sophisticated dishes reinventing Cycladic classics, including a Greek salad made with strawberries and cucumber sorbet, and a slow-cooked lamb accompanied with creamy labneh. *verinahotelsifnos.com*

Rooms with a view
Though Verina Astra opened in 2008 with only seven rooms, seven more were added in 2018 and another two pool suites opened in 2021: each is named after a constellation, encouraging awe-inspiring stargazing at night time. The hotel's infinity pool accentuates the feeling of floating, but it's worth taking the 10-minute shortcut to the rocky, secluded beach underneath.

COASTAL HOTEL
ARISTIDE
Syros

Oana Aristide, her sister Jasmin and her mother Simona were looking for a holiday flat on Syros in 2017 when the estate agent showed them a monumental four-storey building with Doric columns, spiral marble staircases and five-metre-high ceilings. "Ermoupolis was built by wealthy refugees," says Oana, referring to the island's position as a haven for displaced Greeks during the revolution of the 1820s. "They wanted to establish Syros as the main trading point in the Eastern Mediterranean, and so they built to impress: for instance, the town hall is fit for a national capital, not for an island of 25,000 people." The trio decided to take a punt on the house. The renovation took three years and today the Aristide features nine suites, an art gallery, an artists' residence, an award-winning restaurant, two bars and a panoramic roof terrace. "We made minimal changes to the structure," she adds. "This resulted in fewer guest rooms, but it means every single guest can experience the feeling that they are in a palazzo." *hotelaristide.com*

COASTAL HOTEL
ARGINI
Syros

Over seven years of intensive renovation work, surveyor Yiannis Polykretis and his family transformed a listed neoclassical villa, built in 1853, into a luxury hotel. The 200-year-old frescoed ceilings were restored, the bathrooms were lavishly decorated with marble from Greece and Italy, the old doors were refurbished and the floors adorned with oak parquet. No expense or effort was spared with the furnishings: many of them were made by craftsmen in Athens and on Syros. Of the 11 rooms – four suites and seven doubles – the Argini master suite is the most impressive: its detailed ceiling fresco depicts mythical creatures, portraits of Italian and Greek revolutionaries and idyllic landscape scenes. The two former cisterns of the manor house now house a hammam and an indoor pool, while the hotel's Elexis restaurant is located in the courtyard. Here, chef Nikos Stamatis uses island specialities such as fresh fish, *kopanisti* cheese and Cycladic capers to create delicious South Aegean dishes.
arginisyros.gr

COASTAL HOTEL
EKIES
Halkidiki

Like many Thessalonians, Alexandra Efstathiadou has fond memories of holidays in Vourvourou in Sithonia, Halkidiki's middle peninsula. Dubbed the "Hawaii of Greece", this coastal idyll of azure shallows and sandy beaches is a 90-minute drive from the country's second city. In 2001, Efstathiadou inherited a tract of woodland, took a crash course in interior design and began building Ekies, a 76-key retreat overlooking Vourvourou Bay. The eco-conscious resort is alive with the rhythmic buzzing of cicadas. "Nature was here before us, so we tried to create a property that would simply blend in," says Efstathiadou. "I know every tree in the area. Each time one dies, we plant three more." Inside are contemporary design pieces including Scandinavian furniture from Carl Hansen & Søn and Hay, Greek artworks and bespoke textiles made in an atelier in Thessaloniki. "At Ekies, guests feel carefree," says Efstathiadou. "By day two they're walking around barefoot in a swimming costume. That, for me, is freedom."
ekies.gr

AMANZOE
Agios Panteleimonas, Peloponnese

Set on a hill on the Peloponnesian Argolis peninsula, Amanzoe may be over two hours from Athens, but its marble-clad villas and column-lined, Parthenon-like pavilions intentionally nod to the Acropolis. Overlooking the bay of Porto Heli and sitting within Unesco-protected ruins, olive groves and cypresses, the resort is how you might imagine the Mount Olympus of antiquity looked. The guest rooms are designed by American Ed Tuttle with Hellenic simplicity in mind and brought into the 21st century with a minimalist touch. There's yoga in the morning and the honey-oil massages are the highlight at the light-filled, lavender-scented spa.
aman.com/resorts/amanzoe

RURAL HOTEL

KTIMA LEMONIES
Andros

Andros, the northernmost island of the Cyclades, is known for its quiet villages and lush landscapes. If you're heading inland, the pace of life gets even slower. Ktima Lemonies is a 200-year-old farm that's been turned into five beautifully restored units. Architect-owner Adi Biran was keen to preserve the charm of the estate, surrounded by lemon groves and looking towards the distant Aegean. All restoration was carried out with materials from the island for a result that's respectful of historical building methods; whitewashed walls, stone pathways and wooden beams give the place a serene but unstuffy feel. Fresh produce, picked directly from the estate's vegetable patches and fruit trees, goes into the dishes: as does plenty of homegrown olive oil and wine made using grapes from the hotel's vineyard. "The estate is dedicated to preserving the natural environment and cultural legacy of Andros," says Biran with evident pride. "This is part of our dedication to providing guests with a genuine taste of the island." *ktimalemonies.gr*

RURAL HOTEL

METOHI KINDELIS
Chania, Crete

On her return to her native Crete after a career working abroad, Danai Kindeli (*pictured*) took over the running of the guesthouses on her family's estate, Metohi Kindelis, on the southern edge of Chania. "I was travelling so much and working so hard," says Kindeli. "I came back to Crete to recover. I had no intention of staying." When her uncle suggested working with him, she gave it a shot. Her uncle now manages the farmland around the elegant, 16th-century property, with its arches and pink-hued walls. Each of the three guesthouses has its own pool, patio and garden, and feels more like a holiday home than a hotel. *metohi-kindelis.gr*

RURAL HOTEL
APEIROS CHORA
Kato Pedina, Zagori

Driven by a deep connection to their 300-year-old ancestral home, the owners of Apeiros Chora in Zagori restored the family mansion and transformed it into a guesthouse in 2015. Artefacts and items from the building's previous life as a residence are on display, including original Thonet chairs, art deco items and daily utensils. "We have always valued open houses and private gatherings with friends and have a strong personal connection to the property's memories," says Athina Kontouris, the co-owner. "We choose to treat our guests more like family friends," adds her husband, Georgios. *apeiroschora.gr*

Country house
Faced with declining local industries like winemaking and honey farming, the Kontouris family embraced tourism to preserve the property and contribute to the survival of modern Greece's first Unesco-protected cultural landscape (*see page 169*). "We love sharing the rich culture and history of Zagori with our guests," says eighth-generation co-owner Xenofon Kontouris.

RURAL HOTEL
MANNA
Magouliana, Peloponnese

When an abandoned sanatorium in Arcadia came up for auction, Stratis Batagias bought a 50-year lease on it. He first came across it while sneaking off from summer camp as a child. "It was ready to collapse," says Batagias. "But because it was one of the first buildings in Greece to be made with concrete, it had managed to stay standing. But only just." To restore the building, Batagias enlisted Athens-based architects Monogon and K-Studio, who kept its heritage-listed façade and sweeping terrazzo staircase. Since opening, Manna has become popular with Athenians looking for a weekend escape. "The 'Arcadian Ideal' is all about man living in harmony with nature," says Batagias. "Here, you really feel all the seasons very deeply."
mannaarcadia.gr

DISCOVER GREECE | RURAL HOTELS

GRAND FOREST METSOVO
Metsovo, Epirus

The village of Metsovo in northern Greece is a year-round destination popular for its gentle skiing slopes and untouched wilderness. On the edge of the dense, black pine forest, the 62-suite Grand Forest Metsovo is the former family estate of Ellie Barmpagiannis. "The setting prompted us to transform it into a one-of-a-kind boutique hotel," says Barmpagiannis. "It allows guests to connect with nature in a respectful way." Opened in 2013 and designed by Athens-based architect Vaggelis Stylianidis, each suite has uninterrupted views of the mountains and woods. Natural materials complement handcrafted furniture and decor. "I will always return to the mountain to feel grateful and grounded," says Barmpagiannis.
grand-forest.gr

RURAL HOTEL
KINSTERNA
Monemvasia, Peloponnese

Encircled by olive groves and vineyards with views of the Aegean sea in the distance, this 18th-century mansion in the Peloponnesian countryside is a short drive from the seaside town of Monemvasia. "I've always been deeply connected to the history and traditions of this land," says owner Antonis Sgardelis, who grew up in the nearby village of Koulentia and bought the abandoned estate in 2006. Sgardelis restored the property over four years and named it after the well in the courtyard, now filled with water lilies. The hotel makes its own wine, olive oil and honey, and its three restaurants use produce from the gardens. "Our philosophy of self-sufficiency, much like in the old days, is not just a business model but a way to preserve the essence of this historical residence and the region's heritage," he says. Guests are encouraged to take part: there's beekeeping, cooking, and soap and candle-making workshops for those who wish to add to their itinerary of basking in the sun and cooling off in one of the two pools. *kinsternahotel.gr*

RURAL HOTEL
OPORA
Pirgiotika, Peloponnese

Set into the undulating Peloponnese landscape, this guesthouse is a jewel comprising only a handful of self-contained rooms surrounded by olive groves and orange trees. Guests can indulge in days in the shade by the pool and hearty Greek staples from *pastitsio* to *moussaka* made from Naxos beef and gruyère. Konstantinos Markidis – who hails from Athens, where he owns deli-cum-restaurant I Frati in Kifissia – began renovating his family's farmhouse on the 40-hectare property in 2015. Opora, meaning fruit, was inspired by a previous business idea of exporting Greek produce. Instead, Markidis created this quiet retreat. "It's a taste of slow living," he says. "It's a luxury to be in the hills and experience the rhythms of nature." *oporacountryliving.com*

URBAN HOTEL
APOLLO PALM
Athens

Athens has seen a revival in urban hotels. The Apollo Palm is among the best: a 48-key stopover housed in a Bauhaus-style, 1930s police station in an area full of galleries and antique shops. Interiors are by Paris-based designer Mariette Sans-Rival, who knows how to create dramatic spaces given her specialism in opera set design. The rooftop bar has views of the Acropolis and open-air cinema nights and sunset parties with live music can be arranged by request. *apollopalmhotel.com*

URBAN HOTEL
HOTEL GRANDE BRETAGNE
Athens

The Hansen Brothers
Along with his brother Christian, architect Theophil Hansen was also responsible for designing the Academy of Athens, the National Library of Greece and the original Athens University building, three stunning neoclassical structures on Athens' Panepistimiou Street known collectively as the Athenian Trilogy.

Built as a private mansion in the 1840s by Danish architect Theophil Hansen, Hotel Grande Bretagne housed athletes at the first modern Olympic Games in 1896 as well as notable figures such as Baron Pierre de Coubertin, the founder of the modern Olympic movement. "When you walk in, you can feel the history," says general manager Hom Parviz. Yet the 320-room Hotel Grand Bretagne, restored in anticipation of the 2004 Games, feels far from old-fashioned. Modern twists, sophisticated decor and first-class service make the Athenian landmark enduringly popular.
marriott.com/en-us/hotels/athlc

URBAN HOTEL
SHILA
Athens

Tranquil spaces are rare in the Greek capital, so Shila's leafy rooftop garden is a welcome draw, perched above the well-heeled Kolonaki district. This is the sort of discreet gem where you check in for a night and end up staying a week. The building dates to the 1920s and has six suites, each with a private garden or balcony. Faded oriental rugs and rustic stone sinks complement creamy gauze curtains, plush sofas and custom wooden cabinets. "I love exploring the effect of a space on your psyche," says co-founder Eftihia Stefanidi, who also runs Hotel Mona in Psyrri. "Warmth was the key for us." Warmth it has – but the breeze may be what clinches it.
shila-athens.com

URBAN HOTEL
FOUR SEASONS ASTIR PALACE
Athens

The Astir Peninsula south of Athens is just a 30-minute drive from the city centre and its crowning jewel is the Astir Palace. Once the Athenian Riviera's go-to summer resort, hosting everyone from Brigitte Bardot and Frank Sinatra to Richard Nixon and Jackie Kennedy, management was taken over by Four Seasons in 2018 and the 1960s property has since been reinvigorated by an extensive overhaul. Aeter Architects preserved the original buildings and today there are 303 rooms, multiple pools and dining options, 2,000 contemporary Greek artworks – and three private beaches. *fourseasons.com/athens*

Causing Astir
The site for the Four Seasons Astir Palace was first picked out back in the 1950s, when the Greek state earmarked an idyllic spot on the peninsula for an upscale resort, as part of a national drive to promote tourism.

URBAN HOTEL
ON RESIDENCE
Thessaloniki

A stone's throw from Thessaloniki's centuries-old Modiano market, On Residence opened in 2022 on the city's famous waterfront. Designed by Greek architect Jacques Mosse in the 1920s, the plush art deco building – with its impressive high ceilings – was once a hub for Thessaloniki's elite, and home to the storied Olympos Naoussa restaurant that hosted plenty of celebrities in its heyday. The listed building was declared a cultural heritage site in 1993 and was restored to its former glory by Athens and London-based Divercity Architects, Thessaloniki studio Nikiforidis-Cuomo and French interior designer Fabienne Spahn. Think plush drapery, rich gemstone tones and smart light fixtures, lending this modern 60-key hotel a touch of early 20th-century panache. After being shut for over three decades, the Olympos Naoussa restaurant also reopened, with a Mediterranean menu by celebrated head chef Dimitris Tasioulas. The secret courtyard offers a small slice of nature in this concrete-heavy city.
onresidence.gr

Greece has a long history of hosting travellers that goes all the way back to antiquity, but both the country and the hotel trade have evolved rapidly. We speak to three people in the industry about their experiences.

MEET THE EXPERTS

HOTELIER
KOSTIS KARATZAS
The Modernist, Thessaloniki

Hotelier Kostis Karatzas founded The Modernist hotel in Thessaloniki in 2018, before opening an Athenian outpost in 2020. He talks to *Monocle* about running hotels in Greece's two biggest cities and why The Modernist is about more than just hotels.

What's the key to great hospitality?
It's about harnessing a relationship with people and the city that looks different for each guest. Hospitality is about being authentic and honest. A lot of hotels concentrate on keeping guests within the hotel, but we want to offer a good coffee in the morning and then get people out to explore what the city has to offer.

What's the ethos of The Modernist?
I wanted to create a brand rather than just a hotel. Though our core business is hotels, we have a café next door that is open to the guests and the public because I want people to feel part of it.

How different is it running a hotel in different cities?
It's the same brand but with different details. Our hotels are suited to their surroundings. They reflect the individual energies of their cities. We like to add to the neighbourhoods we're in as well as creating somewhere for travellers and locals to interact and feel they belong.
themodernisthotels.com

HOTELIER
NAUSIKA GEORGIADOU
Skinopi Lodge, Milos

Nausika Georgiadou is the founder and owner of Skinopi Lodge. When she first came to Milos in the 1980s aged 18, there were no phones; passengers alighting from the Piraeus ferry were greeted on the dock by islanders carrying room-to-let signs. First she took an old ruin with a breathtaking view and turned it into a B&B. Then she spent over a decade acquiring a seafront property and in 2016 opened the five-star hotel she runs today.

What sets Skinopi apart?
It is my dream of what hospitality in Greece should be. People slow down here and rediscover the healing powers of silence and nature.

What were the challenges when you first opened?
Everything for the construction had to be shipped from Athens. Even finding this hidden spot in the first place was difficult, as was securing the necessary permits. Then, it was a challenge to find trained staff. But being a five-star property, expectations are very high and obviously meeting them is our top priority.

What was the design inspiration?
We brought in some traditional elements, even though the design is modern. Our large open living spaces and wooden shutters reflect the fishermen's homes in our cove, and because summer in the islands is so special, I included outdoor cooking and bathing spaces.

What do you see as the future of hospitality at Skinopi Lodge?
To capitalise on the beauty of the landscape, the human scale of our small country, the warm people, and the deep layers of our history and culture.
skinopi.com

HOTELIER
AGAPI SBOKOU
Phaea Hospitality, Crete

Agapi Sbokou is the co-owner and CEO of the Phaea group. Her late father, Yannis Sbokou, founded the business in 1976, and today Agapi and her sister Costantza are at the helm. The group owns four hotels on Crete, with more planned, including a collaboration with Rosewood for the latter's first project in Greece.

Where do you draw inspiration from?
From our father, our heritage, from the island where we grew up and where the business started. Hospitality to us means treating a guest as if they're staying in your own home. You could say that this is inherently Greek, but even more so Cretan.

How do you balance Phaea's successful legacy with progress?
Another thing our father instilled in us is the importance of consistency without complacency; trying to maintain high standards while continuing to innovate. This balance between tradition and authenticity is something that continues to guide us today.

What does luxury mean to you?
The word "luxury" is very often abused. To me, it's about an experience that transcends the ordinary. It's about creating special moments of pure joy and serenity that allow you to connect with yourself.

What is next for Phaea?
We want to evolve, together with our guests, towards a kinder and more immersive version of travel. This means helping guests form deeper connections with nature and the local community, and focusing on how design can help allow for those connections to happen.
phaea.com

New takes on Greece's hearty cuisine are taking inspiration from the country's past and the spontaneous joys of the village taverna. Here is our list of the best culinary talent in the land.

DRINKING & DINING

No image embodies Greek food culture better than a raucous group of friends relishing shared *mezedes* (small dishes) to the sound of clinking glasses. Thanks to its excellent raw materials and simplicity, Greek cuisine has long been recognised for harnessing the flavours and benefits of the Mediterranean diet. Now a younger generation of chefs has capitalised on the quality of the nation's produce and added worldly creativity to traditional recipes to create innovative dishes. Even simple tavernas (the cornerstone of Greece's gastronomic identity) marinate fish in tangy fruits and herbs to put together ceviches. From truffles to saffron, beans to wine – and, of course, oil and honey – the country is brimming with great ingredients and you'll find many on offer at a lively neighbourhood *laiki* (farmers' market). Indulge in seafood, goat meat and pulses on the islands and warm up with meaty stews and pies in the mountains; let us offer a sample of this variety in the pages to come.

THE EDIT

1 **Restaurants**
From sophisticated urban dining rooms to sun-dappled island terraces.

2 **Tavernas**
The hub of Greek daily life.

3 **Bakeries**
Spots to get your fresh bread, flaky pastries and more.

4 **Sweet treats**
Toothsome delights from *bougatsa* to ice cream.

5 **Cafés & speciality coffee**
Flat whites, freddo espressos and more caffeine fixes.

6 **Bars**
Aperitifs and nightcap venues. *Yiá mas!*

7 **Drink producers**
Dedicated specialists producing uniquely Greek bottles.

8 **Food retailers**
The best places to stock up on the tastiest provisions.

9 **Markets**
Where the community comes together to find the best ingredients.

10 **The experts**
Three insiders tell us how to get ahead in the business.

RESTAURANT
TAVERNA TON FILON
Athens

Taverna ton Filon may give the impression of having been around forever but in truth it only opened in 2023. In a dimly lit dining room with white tablecloths and café curtains, Ton Filon (meaning "friend's taverna") offers a compact, can't-go-wrong menu paired with Greek wines from small producers. Chef Yannis Mousios cooks with an easy hand, serving up classic dishes that vary almost daily, depending on the ingredients available and his whimsy. The repertoire includes different takes on *gigantes*, typical baked beans, as well as *moussakas* and dips.
Argous 66, Athina

Back to life
Chef Yannis Mousios – previously of Athenian dining institution Seychelles – and sommelier Giorgos Kontorizos (*pictured, on left, with Mousios*), who has poured wines at Michelin-starred establishments, took over this locale, in the residential Kolonos neighbourhood, after it had been abandoned for over a decade and returned it to its former glory as a homey 1950s taverna.

RESTAURANT
FITA
Athens

The southern neighbourhood of Neos Kosmos was an unlikely choice when Fita opened in 2019. But this minimalist gastro taverna run by three chefs now has an established following – and a menu that varies nearly every day. "Everything is freshly cooked and although we have certain standard dishes, we vary according to the season and the catch of the day," says chef Dimitris Dimitriadis (*pictured*). Wooden Viennese chairs and marble tabletops are reminiscent of old Athenian *kafeneia* (traditional cafés). Patrons can eat on the terrace or inside, where an elevated counter offers a chance to observe the open kitchen. Dishes primarily revolve around fish, like the grey mullet tartare with cucumber, purslane and lemon-oil sauce or the beetroot nigiri topped with smoked eel and greens. "Simple homemade dishes are hard to find nowadays, but we add our creative touches," explains Dimitriadis. Try the *stifado* stew made with wine and rooster or their *kotsi*: pork shanks in beer sauce with grilled cabbage.
Ntourm 1, Athens

RESTAURANT
AKRA
Athens

Giannis Loukakis and Spyros Pediaditakis met when the latter was working as a pastry chef at two-Michelin-starred restaurant Spondi. Akra, their joint venture, opened in Athens' Pangrati neighbourhood in 2023. It rapidly became a favourite with Athenians for its friendly atmosphere and exceptional cuisine. "We find our fruit and vegetables at the local organic market and update the menu daily," says Pediaditakis. Dishes are grilled in front of punters and are best enjoyed with a glass of Greek wine from the small but thoughtful wine list. The dessert menu, which features delights such as a memorable caramelised milk tart, is the undeniable cherry on top.
Amynta 12, Athens

RESTAURANT
CAFÉ AVISSINIA
Athens

Avissinias Square is home to a famous flea market so it's no surprise that this classic Athenian stop-in should feel like a cabinet of curiosities. Chef Ketty Koufonikola-Touros created the café in 1985, back when it was the first of its kind in the commerce-centred neighbourhood. The roof terrace has excellent views of the Acropolis and hosts live folk music from September to June. The café is famous for its indulgent and comforting dishes, from cheesy aubergines to an exquisite spin on *dakos* (rye rusk with freshly grated tomatoes and cream cheese) – and the best fried potatoes in Athens. *cafeavissinia.net*

À la carte adornment
Chef Ketty Koufonikola-Touros has been collecting decorative pieces from the antique stalls and shops all around Avissinias Square ever since the café opened, amassing an eclectic mix of tapestries, sculptures, odd mirrors, ceramics and oil paintings to decorate the space.

GALLINA
Athens

A newcomer to the prim Koukaki neighbourhood, Gallina is a treat not only for diners but for art and design lovers, too. Its elegant and bold mid-century aesthetic spans all shades of brown, from the marble tabletops to the terrazzo flooring. The food is similarly confident: chef Pavlos Kyriakis combines Greek, French and Scandinavian cuisine into dishes such as turbot in assyrtiko wine sauce and rotisserie chicken with miso beurre blanc. "It's modern but classic at the same time," says Vasileios Bakasis, CEO of Gallina's parent group. "It's comfort food with a fine-dining spin." *gallina.gr*

Gallina: style kitchen
The restaurant's striking interior design comes courtesy of LOT Office for Architecture. They gave pride of place to an immense wall-mounted tapestry by Jannis Varelas, a piece originally created for an exhibition at The Breeder gallery (*see page 136*).

RESTAURANT
LINOU SOUMPASIS K SIA
Athens

A well-lit, minimalist white cube, Linou Soumpasis k Sia stands out on an unassuming, graffiti-sprayed street in the central district of Psyrri. Opened in late 2021, it's probably the finest example of the "neo-taverna" style that has emerged in Greece over the past few years – one that is oft-replicated, yet rarely as successfully realised as here. Its founders, Myrsini Linou and Giorgios Soumpasis (after whom the restaurant is named) brought in chef Lukas Mailer from the island of Lemnos to take over the kitchen. The eclectic seasonal menu uses organic, fresh ingredients for versions of the classics that will surprise the well-initiated: Mailer's Greek salad swaps feta for brie. Dishes are essential and stripped back but pack a flavourful punch – the revolving menu features the likes of juicy skewers of tuna, sardines lying on a bed of saucy beans, and moreish roasted courgettes stuffed with shrimp. Pick a table in the bright and airy space that gives you a view onto the busy open kitchen.
linousoumpasis.gr

RESTAURANT
WINE IS FINE
Athens

Wine bar-cum-bistro Wine is Fine makes the most of its location a short walk from the vast Athens Municipal Market. "When we run out of an ingredient, I just run to the market," says Athenian chef Stavros Chrysafidis. "It's like our pantry." The business opened in 2023 in a former door-handle shop on bustling Vyssis Street, and is run by Chrysafidis alongside co-founders and Parisian natives Rafael Wallon-Brownstone and Thomas Brengou. Although the venue has strong French influences, it constantly reinvents itself and the trio are keen to draw on Chrysafidis' experience working in kitchens in Japan, London and Basel.
wineisfine.gr

RESTAURANT
AKTI
Vouliagmeni

South of Athens in the quiet seaside town of Vouliagmeni, Akti perches on an old pier jutting into the bay. "Growing up in Vouliagmeni, [this spot] was my brother Giagos' and my favourite," says Thodoris Agiostratitis, who co-owns Akti with his sibling. "It was our dream to bring it back to life." It was Giagos, an architect, who redesigned the building – it opened in 2021. Inside, the hum of diners talking over plates of amberjack sashimi, fried langoustines and grilled grouper makes for a cosy atmosphere. Outside, tables sprawl onto the pier itself: lit in the evenings with strings of lights, it enjoys sunset views over the water.
aktirestaurant.com

RESTAURANT
CASA FISTIKI
Antiparos

A 20-minute drive south on the coastal road from Antiparos's harbour will deliver you to the sleepy bay of Agios Georgios, lying opposite the uninhabited island nature reserve of Despotiko. Swiss-Dutch architect Caroline Favre and aviation entrepreneur Chris Marich (*pictured*), fell in love with this spot on their first visit to Antiparos in 2023. "We didn't know anyone on the island and we didn't speak Greek," says Favre. Nevertheless, the couple decided to realise their dream here, and today offer upscale Mexican cuisine made from fresh Mediterranean ingredients for a clientele of barefoot gourmets. Favre designed the furniture for the high-end establishment herself and collaborated with chefs Joaquin Cardoso and Alonso Lara to devise the menu, inspired by having lived in Mexico City for five years and her travels around the country. Signature dishes include corn ribs, tuna *tostadas*, Josper-grilled butterflied fish and for those with a sweet tooth, *churros* with chocolate ice cream and chocolate sauce. *casafistiki.com*

RESTAURANT
MAIAMI
Chania, Crete

Maiami is a laid-back restaurant and gallery run by ceramicist-proprietor Alexandra Manousakis (*pictured*). The Greek-American had been living in New York when she stumbled across the structure, formerly a restaurant called Maiami (the Greek spelling for Miami, which she decided to keep). "I kept thinking that this could be my little patch of Crete," she says. It became her studio and eventually a brasserie serving her favourite foods, from watermelon salad to prawn and ouzo pasta. Manousakis's playful designs are sold in a gallery shop, but are also used on the restaurant's crockery, set on pastel tables in a nod to its nominal Floridian origins. *maiamichania.com*

RESTAURANT
THALASSINO AGERI
Chania, Crete

A different tan

Thalassino Ageri has been drawing
Cretan vacationers since it opened in
1983. It is in a neighbourhood filled
with crumbling but charming buildings
that were once leather factories in the
mid-19th century.

Only a handful of steps from the saltwater-splashed rocks of
Chania's port, Thalassino Ageri is a decades-old upscale
taverna known for its fresh fish. In this part of town, the area
of Tabakaria, you'll find regulars – residents catching up on
their work days while spinning *komboloi* (the traditional worry
beads) or summering Athenian families dancing through
dinner – who know that the tables are best reserved from
19.00 onwards. The menu features seasonal dishes and
freshly caught grilled fish, including snapper, red mullet,
squid or crispy sardines.
thalasino-ageri.gr

RESTAURANT

THE VENETIAN WELL
Corfu

Wine enthusiast Yiannis Vlachos transformed a tired bar hidden away in Corfu's old town into one of the island's most beloved establishments when he opened The Venetian Well with his partner Eirini. Chef Spyros Agious (*pictured*) takes inspiration from his grandmother's cooking to redefine Corfiot cuisine: the restaurant serves up exceptional tasting menus drawing from flavours the Venetians introduced over 500 years ago when they colonised the island. Try the rooster *pastitsada* (a traditional Greek pasta dish) spiked with cinnamon or leave it to chef Agious and the expert sommeliers to deliver a meal you are unlikely to forget. *venetianwell.gr*

RESTAURANT
PESKESI
Heraklion, Crete

Hidden in a narrow passageway in the old town of Heraklion, Peskesi offers Cretan cuisine with a farm-to-table ethos and the desire to revive forgotten recipes. Panagiotis Magganas opened the restaurant in 2014 with ingredients on its menu sourced from his own farm or other local producers. The dining room is set inside a restored mansion formerly owned by a sea captain, with a terrace draped in vines and interiors decked with rustic wooden tables. Try the classic Cretan snails, slow-cooked chickpeas or sweet-and-sour *tzoulamas* pie with rice, cheese, almonds, raisins and cinnamon.
peskesicrete.gr

Lay of the land
In the late 1990s, Magganas established a 12-hectare organic farm in nearby Hersonissos. Today, the land is home to farm animals, produces over 120 varieties of vegetables, fruits, olives and herbs via biodynamic and regenerative methods, and also hosts culinary classes.

RESTAURANT
TECHNE
Hydra

After 10 years working in London as an investment banker, Athenian-born Jason Barios relocated to Hydra in 2016 to open a restaurant with his friend, chef Yannis Michalopoulos (*pictured*). "Back then, it was rare to find modern Greek cuisine on the island," says Barios. "We have great respect for the traditions of the tavernas, but we wanted to offer a bit of a twist because we're influenced by the Mediterranean's different cuisines and how these speak to Greece's native flavours." For starters it's *dolmadakia*: vine leaves stuffed with white anchovies, smoked yoghurt and tomato jam; followed by grilled pata negra pork loin with sage gnocchi, mushrooms and aged graviera cheese; all accompanied by Greek craft beer. Still, Techne's most distinguishing feature is the beauty of its location. Outside Hydra's only town, the path to the restaurant is deliberately unmarked and unlit. "Hydra is a car-free island, so you have to put in a bit of effort," says Barios. The payoff is a decidedly intimate setup soundtracked by the soporific sound of Saronic waves. *techne-hydra.com*

RESTAURANT
MPLE KANARINI
Kalamata, Peloponnese

After honing his skills at top culinary destinations across Greece and Europe – such as Amanzoe (*see page 30*) and the two-Michelin-starred Les Cols in Catalunya – chef Konstantinos Vasiliadis returned to his hometown of Kalamata. Today, his kitchen celebrates the bounty of the southern Peloponnese. "We source from small local businesses, fishermen, and farmers," he says. "We've also created a small garden across the street for growing some of our vegetables." The menu changes daily, offering contemporary dishes that honour Greek traditions: signature favourites include stuffed courgette flowers in tomato sauce and sourdough noodles with *sfela* cheese, fresh tomatoes and basil, served on handmade plates from Athens-based Antigoni Ceramics. The serene ambience, dreamed up by interior designer Anna Patriarchea, blends natural wood and marble with details in pastel colours. "The central axis is undoubtedly the open kitchen, where the chef engages directly with diners," says Patriarchea. *Kritis 34, Kalamata*

RESTAURANT
LELA'S TAVERNA
Kardamyli, Peloponnese

Giorgos Giannakeas has been running this restaurant since taking over from his mother Lela in 1983, more recently with the help of his wife and son. "She was a talented cook," says Giannakeas, who was born in the house that today hosts the dining room. "Nothing fancy, she just liked slow-cooking and very tasty dishes." He has now brought Greece-born, French-trained chef Stathis Bakas on board. This means the menu has been updated to showcase contemporary options, such as *xerosfeli* fried cheese with mulberry jam and seabass ceviche with citrus, radishes and orange-hibiscus sorbet, but the taverna's sense of easy hospitality has not changed.
lelastaverna.com

RESTAURANT
DILAILA
Lipsi

Home to just 700 people, Lipsi is a small and intimate island in the Dodecanese. Life here revolves around the harbour, where traditional tavernas and small shops line the waterfront, but for an unforgettable meal, head to Katsadia beach. There you'll find Dilaila, a laid-back beach bar-restaurant where colourful, wooden chairs sit under a handwoven shade canopy. Owned by Lipsi-born Christodoulos Gampieris since 1993, this seaside gem enjoys views over a stunning bay. Gampieris learnt his trade working on merchant ships and together with his wife Dimitra Gabrani he serves delicious dishes from June to September to a loyal clientele, many of whom arrive by boat. Their menu celebrates the island's fresh produce, with favourites like the fiery "crazy feta", accompanied by a tangy Greek salad with pickled caper leaves, a beetroot tzatziki and grilled aubergine with homemade hummus. Every month, the full-moon gatherings at Dilaila are legendary and are a celebration of relaxed island life.
Lipsi 850 01

RESTAURANT
DISKO ROMEIKO
Litochoro, Central Macedonia

RESTAURANT
RIZES
Mykonos

With profound love and respect for their *rizes* (roots), the Zouganeli family brought a Mykonian village back to life with this rustic but chic restaurant. The kitchen uses fresh, seasonal ingredients for hearty stews and fragrant herb-infused pies. Cheese and wine are also produced on site following time-honoured techniques. The Zouganelis also offer cooking workshops, and can organise leisurely picnics accompanied by horses carrying basketfuls of favourites from *souvlaki* to fresh salad from the garden. Five cosy bedrooms are also available for those wanting to bed down for a night away from busy Mykonos town.
rizesmykonos.com

Owners Maritina Daskalaki (*pictured*) and Nikos Evgenis turned this old sawmill near Mount Olympus into a place patrons can fill up ahead of their climb to the abode of the gods, or simply linger. "We have *mezedes*, but customers come for coffee in the morning and can have cocktails in the evening. People just enjoy hanging out here," says Daskalaki. The name describes some of the attributes of this modern *kafeneio*: the music ranges from disco to Balearic and some of the wines on its list are made from Cretan romeiko grapes. The owners' personal items – from portraits drawn by a client, to a Berlin coffee poster – give this spot an idiosyncratic style.
Faraggi Enipea, Litochoro

RESTAURANT
PAPAIOANNOU
Mykonos

Seafood is plentiful in Greece but Papaioannou's Mykonos outpost is one of its top purveyors. "We chose to open in Agios Stefanos, one of the quieter areas of Mykonos away from the party crowds," says founder Giorgos Papaioannou. Signature dishes include raw plates, sardines, grilled squid and steamed dusky grouper, as well as his legendary *taramasalata*. Papaioannou brought in Athens-based designers Stones & Walls to create a cliffside oasis with accents of azure blue and white. "The setting itself is enough to inspire you to travel to this side of Mykonos," says Papaioannou.

Island odyssey
This Mykonos restaurant is the latest addition to the Papaioannou hospitality stable and the first outside of the Athens region. Its first location opened in the early 1990s in Piraeus with Papaioannou himself at the grill.

RESTAURANT
THE SQUIRREL
Nikiti, Halkidiki

One of Greece's most lauded dining establishments is hidden away inside The Danai, a five-star resort on the Halkidiki beachfront. The Squirrel has only five tables set out on a terrace and diners are treated to a 10 to 12-course tasting menu by chef Vasilis Mouratidis. Signature dishes include: smoked mussels in pine tree with asparagus and vin jaune sauce with aged parmesan; and glazed cod with leek velouté, lemon purée and beurre blanc sauce with ossetra caviar. Shaded by pine trees and overlooking the Aegean, the service is unlikely to be disrupted by anything except the restaurant's namesake treetop critter. Make sure to book ahead.
thedanai.com/dining/the-squirrel

RESTAURANT
CANTINA ANALOGUE
Syros

Cantina Analogue is Cyclades-native artist Christos Artemis' vision of a restaurant-cum-wine bar, set inside a warehouse. It's a lofty arrangement, with eclectic décor to fill it. Wooden beams prop up the ceiling and tall potted plants dot the room, overlooked by an impressive floor-to-ceiling peacock mural. Through a network of Cycladian partners, the restaurant fills its pantry with regional specialties such as semi-wild artichokes from neighbouring Tinos, where Artemis grew up. If you're a movie lover, come for the occasional summer screenings – or, if you're musically inclined, take the old-school jukebox for a spin.

+30 2281 302412

RESTAURANT
CANTINA
Sifnos

The cantina of this restaurant's name is a small cellar and pantry used to ferment, cure and dry produce for its satisfying, imaginative dishes. "It's our lab," says founder Georgios Samoilis, a former molecular biologist who founded the spot in 2020, showcasing the island's produce. "The island is famous for chickpeas, goat's cheese and fish; but working closely with farmers we have recovered some interesting seeds when it comes to vegetables and pulses." Running this venture is far from easy – there's no direct road and 100 steps separate the kitchen from the closest access. But the location is better for it: a bohemian, laid-back terrace overlooking the bay, below the medieval citadel of Kastro. While Samoilis also runs the sun-dappled Pelicanos in Faros beach, here the ruffled atmosphere only adds to elegant but unfussy dishes like juicy amberjack *souvlaki* with sour cream, a crispy chickpea panisse and some exceptional fish crudos. "Every day you get a picture of what's going on produce-wise on the island," says Samoilis.
cantinasifnos.gr

RESTAURANT
TIFFANY'S × 1905
Thessaloniki

For a city with such historic gastronomic traditions, Tiffany's × 1905, a Parisian-style bistro with a Cretan heart, feels like a novelty. But the restaurant-cum-wine bar follows another institution named Tiffany's that occuopied the same building for four decades before closing in 2013. "We didn't want to copy the original but to invent a modern remaking," says restaurateur Nikolaos Nyfoudis. As the city's first wine-forward restaurant, Tiffanys offers 600 labels from everywhere from Naxos to Austria's blaufränkisch. Interior designer Nikos Letsas's clean blue-and-white interiors provide a modern twist on the Greek taverna, but the tongue-in-cheek posters by Turin-based graphic designer Gianluca Cannizzo best show the restaurant's unstuffy attitude. On the menu is *kontosouvli* (chunks of pork roasted on a spit), pickled artichokes from Tinos and braised lamb with strained yoghurt. For dessert, it's *kiounefe*: a pastry shell filled with mozzarella and hard Greek cheese, cooked slowly and drizzled with syrup and pistachios. *tiffanys1905.gr*

RESTAURANT
SYNTROFI
Thessaloniki

Syntrofi (from *syntrofia*, meaning company) is the second opening in Thessaloniki for chef-restaurateur Giannis Loukakis. It might not be easy to find – down a cobbled alley close to the old port – but its modern Greek fare and smooth jazz soundtrack prove to be hugely rewarding. With only outdoor seating, Syntrofi serves a daily menu of 13 *meze*-style plates informed by the seasons: think tortellini stuffed with *arseniko* goat's cheese from Naxos; black pork terrine with aubergine cream and wilted greens; and tomato mopped up with homemade wholemeal sourdough.
Doxis 9, Thessaloniki

Local heroes
Loukakis's zero-waste, nose-to-tail philosophy echoes that of his original seafood-oriented restaurant, Mourga (*see page 64*). He makes a point of working exclusively with small-batch producers from Thessaloniki and the nearby towns of Epanomi and Serres. Co-owner Alexandros Barbounakis selected the lengthy wine list, with exclusively natural wines sourced from all over Greece.

RESTAURANT
MOURGA
Thessaloniki

Thessaloniki is historically considered the nation's food capital, but in 2021 Unesco made it official by designating it a city of gastronomy. Mourga is a discrete seafood spot that opened in 2017 on quiet Christopoulou Street. Chef and founder Giannis Loukakis puts as much emphasis on salad and natural wine as he does on fresh fish in his low-key, taverna-like setting. Ingredients sourced from the city's organic markets end up in classic dishes such as a reimagined *souvlaki*; lemony king prawns are roasted on the spit, while cuttlefish is sliced raw into tagliata and buoyed in a frothy lemon broth.
+30 231 026 8826

RESTAURANT
TO THALASSAKI
Tinos

Chef Antonia Zarpa (*pictured below*) is totally self-taught. But running this restaurant by the water of Ysternia Bay for over two decades with her husband Aris has turned her into one of the Cyclades' most accomplished cooks. Her cuisine is imaginative and features dishes like her *xerolithia* – a layered salad of tomato jelly, aubergine and courgette inspired by the island's dry-stone walls – or Tinian cheese accompanied by pollen and roasted nuts. Her breezy terrace routinely attracts punters from neighbouring islands, who'll come on boats just to enjoy lunch in this relaxed spot. "When people come here, they feel grounded," she says. "It's a special location."
Ysternia Bay, Tinos

RESTAURANT

KANELA & GARYFALLO
Vitsa

When Vassilis Katsoupas (*pictured right*) opened a mushroom-led restaurant in 2005 near Vikos gorge in northwest Greece, he turned heads. To Katsoupas, fungi were a natural wonder, so he put them in the spotlight. In a 100-year-old building in the village of Vitsa, Katsoupas – who trained in his family's Athens restaurant before cooking for many years in Canada – uses over 30 varieties including truffles, morels, chanterelles and shiitake grown at his farm. He cooks them with delicious dishes featuring local meat, fish and dairy produce, inspiring more restaurants to give mushrooms greater respect.
kanela-garyfallo.gr

Mistaken mycology
Residents in Zagori have been wary of foraged mushrooms in the past and many considered them inedible. Despite them being plentiful in the region, fungi have not traditionally been used as ingredients in Greek dishes, in contrast with many other European cuisines.

TAVERNAS
Heart of the community

From Corfu to Kastellorizo, across the length and breadth of Greece, with its wildly different landscapes, dialects and dances, the taverna is a cultural lynchpin that embodies all that it is to be Greek. With red geraniums or fuchsia bougainvillaea exploding from old feta vats, elderly wooden chairs and walls lined with faded photographs, worn-out *bouzoukia* or hanging pumpkins, this institution is more than just a place to have a meal. In Greek culture, they are a place to come home to. Embodying the very essence of the concept of *filoxenia* (showing kindness to strangers), the taverna is a dining room in which locals and travellers eat side by side.

More relaxed than a regular restaurant, the Greek taverna has a cheerful element of the slapdash about it. Instead of tablecloths, the protocol calls for a sheet of paper, often printed with the establishment's name, a kitsch note of welcome or perhaps anchors, ropes and other nautical iconography in biro-ink blue. In the most traditional spots, you won't even receive a menu: instead, the waiter will reel off the *piata imeras* (daily dishes) directly from memory, adding to the insouciant ambience of the place. It will feel as though you have been invited into a Greek home, with the best of each region's cuisine served up according to the season and sourced fresh from the garden or nearby producers.

2

3

Keep it in the family

Tavernas are usually family affairs, with matriarchs in the kitchen and more youthful, sprightly members out front – some of them not yet old enough to drink the alcohol they're serving, depending on the region you're visiting and how relaxed they are in policing laws and regulations.

1

4 5

1 Ntounias Taverna, Drakona, Crete
2 Restaurant Chic, Folegandros
3 Simple, but delicious
4 Meals are intended to be shared
5 The locals have seen it all
6 The more friends, the better
7 Interior design by accretion

6 7

KORA
Athens

RED JANE
Chania, Crete

Cretan hotelier Nikos Tsepetis (*see page 19*) opened this bakery in 2023 after stumbling upon a former foundry in Chania's city centre. He enlisted the help of designer Michael Anastassiades to create a minimalist, marble-adorned space serving up some of the best pastries on the island and a bread menu created by Eyal Schwartz, formerly of London's acclaimed E5 Bakehouse. Fresh sourdough is constantly unloaded from the ovens, but we recommend picking up a *koulouri* (bagel-shaped bread coated in sesame seeds) stuffed with *mizithra* cheese and smoked salmon, alongside a flat white made with beans from Red Jane's own roastery next door. *Kidonias 101, Chania*

For Athens-born Maria Alafouzou and Ianthi Michalaki, what was missing from their hometown was the perfect sourdough loaf. That's why they decided to open Kora, the Greek capital's first sourdough-specialist bakery. At the foot of Lycabettus Hill, in the upscale neighbourhood of Kolonaki, the outpost was previously one of the city's most popular gay clubs but had lain empty for a decade. With the help of local studio En-Route Architecture, the space has been transformed into a yellow and white-fronted spot with floor-to-ceiling windows filled with crusty loaves, flaky croissants and sticky cinnamon rolls.
korabakery.com

72H

Thessaloniki

Formed as the bakery arm of Ergon, the food retailer founded in Thessaloniki in 2008 (*see page 85*), 72H is named for the number of hours its sourdough ferments for. Its bakers prioritise ancient leavening techniques and hand-knead its dough, making for a crunchy exterior and pillowy texture. As well as bouncy loaves flavoured with chocolate, turmeric or beetroot, there are sumptuous honey-drizzled viennoiseries stuffed with spinach, feta and za'atar, highly imaginative *boureki* (potato and courgette pie) and matcha and apricot *babka*.
ergonfoods.com

Bread for success
There are a few 72H locations around Thessaloniki. The first opening was inside the Modiano covered market (*see page 159*) but more recently the mini-chain has expanded to the hip Paleon Patron Germanou neighbourhood and beyond the city's borders into Athens.

SWEET TREATS
AFOI ASIMAKOPOULOI
Athens

Asimakopouloi patisserie has been an Athenian mainstay since it was founded in 1915. Each day begins with deliveries of fresh cow's and sheep's milk, brought in from small farms. The team then starts creating products ranging from rice puddings and *galaktoboureko* (a semolina custard pie), to mango pastry cakes and *tsoureki* (a sweet bread). "We've modernised over the decades, experimenting with new recipes. But our aim is always the same: use the best ingredients and work in keeping with Greece's history of pastry making," says Vasilis Asimakopoulos, a third-generation baker who works alongside sister Jane, father Dimitris and uncle Thanasis. *asimakopouloi.com*

SWEET TREATS
CAKE BOUTIQUE
Corfu

Ageliki Agathou and Evangelos Kyriazis' dessert shop in Corfu's Old Town offers an international take on traditional sweet Greek fare. "I wanted to combine French patisserie traditions with flavours I love," says Agathou. Working with businesses like Dr Kavvadia's Organic Farm (*see page 81*), Cake Boutique whips up creations such as the delicate *ladolemono* macaron, using olive oil gel and lemon jam. Meanwhile, figs are brought from Lesvos to play a starring role in the team's award-winning macaron with spiced fig pie, Cretan sour cheese and Corfiot *noumboulo*. Make sure to also try the chocolate mousse on a crunchy salted-caramel base. *Delvinioti 1, Corfu*

SWEET TREATS
SELECT
Ioannina

Up in the north of Greece, near the Albanian border, Vasiliki Kaskanis and her husband run Select, the oldest *bougatsa* shop in Ioannina. On the city's busiest street, people queue all day for one of two flavours of pies – feta cheese or custard cream made with cow's milk; though it's the sweet version that's the star. The traditional recipe is sacred to the couple: they opened their hole-in-the-wall space in 1964 as young adults, only now passing it down to their daughter and son-in-law who had to quickly learn not to roll out the filo with a pin but instead to stretch it out by hand before throwing it in the air.
Andrea Papandreou 2, Ioannina

SWEET TREATS
DJANGO GELATO
Syros

Syros-based Django Gelato was founded in 2005 and exclusively uses natural ingredients. "It isn't easy to find real, natural ice cream, but our shop feels like an experimental artist's studio," says owner Konstantinos Karakatsanis (*pictured left*). "We collaborate with beekeepers and organic farmers, and source local produce like melons and figs." Though the range of flavours is extensive, Karakatsanis says customers have a particular liking for the pistachio. "I don't have a favourite ingredient – I love to research all their properties," he says. You can also find Django's ice cream at its second home in Athens.
djangogelato.com

SPECIALITY COFFEE
ANANA
Athens

Roam Athens' centre and you'll still come across many shops that maintain an old Athenian atmosphere. Anana opened when the city was still emerging from the financial crisis: here, you'll sip speciality coffee made with beans harvested within the last four months and roasted in-house. In a 1930s building that formerly housed a *kombologadiko* (worry-bead) shop, Anana spans a charming courtyard and terrazzo-floored interiors. In an effort to preserve this increasingly rare, vintage atmosphere, owner Panagotis Xilas decided to minimise aesthetic interventions. "We didn't want it to be noisy visually," he says of the design.
Praxitelous 33, Athens

SPECIALITY COFFEE
THEORIST
Rethymno, Crete

Entrepreneurs Giannis and Iakovos Kontarakis enlisted architect Eleftheria Pyroudi to design Theorist Café in 2023. With its whiter-than-white tile façade and wooden outdoor tables, the bright and breezy café-cum-library has a hint of Scandinavian minimalism about it. The book shelves can host up to 1,000 volumes that are free to look through. Rethymno is known for being a lively university town, though pop-up markets and events have made this spot a go-to for all residents. The menu is simple but effective and ranges from Japanese-inspired sandos to mushroom burgers, cinnamon buns and yoghurt bowls with fruit and chia seeds.
theorist.livemenu.gr

SPECIALITY COFFEE
EPTA
Syros

In Ermoupoli, you'll spot Epta's logo on many takeaway cups – a reflection of the fact it is considered among the island's best coffee. In a shaded passage off the main square, inside a former blacksmith's, this breakfast spot is recognisable by its elegant glass doorway, high ceilings, marble and exposed brickwork. Inside, a crystal chandelier pays homage to the city's distinct neoclassical architecture. Founders Giorgios Prokopis and Sissy Louka, originally from Ioannina on the mainland, fell in love with Syros and wanted to create a relaxed hangout in town. Though the menu features brunch classics, the house speciality is pancakes, both sweet and savoury.

Peloponnisou 7, Ermoupoli, Syros

SPECIALITY COFFEE
FATHER COFFEE & VINYL
Thessaloniki

DJ and record collector Christos Exarchopoulos learned how to combine coffee, wine and music in a single space from the listening bars of Berlin. The Thessalonian lived in the German capital for six years before returning in 2020 to set up Father Coffee & Vinyl with two friends. "In the 1990s, Thessaloniki was known as the music capital of Greece," says Exarchopoulos. Upstairs, collectors can find anything from Balearic disco and Afro jazz to electronica and Brazilian funk. The selection of over 1,000 records changes monthly and is hand-picked by Exarchopoulos himself. Audiophiles connect over coffee roasted by regional micro-roastery Pianeta Gusto, or a glass of natural wine from an experimental Mount Olympus winery. When it comes to his own taste, Exarchopoulos has a soft spot for David Bowie, British singer Sade and American composer Sun Ra. "I have more than 4,000 records at home," says Exarchopoulos. "Father Coffee & Vinyl is just an extension of my own collection."

Stratigou Kallari 9, Thessaloniki

BAR
GALAXY
Athens

One of the oldest bars in Athens, Galaxy opened in 1972. It was originally decorated by a set and costume designer and has barely changed since. A leather-edged counter runs along the narrow space and the wooden-panelled walls are crowded with cheerful portraits of local and foreign personalities. "Everything here is low profile and discreet, and we strive for our service to complement this classic decor," says owner Yiannis Alabanos, whose son now works behind the bar. Drinks are served with complimentary cheese, olives and toasted bread with olive oil. Try the dry martini, margarita or choose a single malt whisky accompanied by smoked pork.
Stadiou 10, Athens

BAR
MATERIA PRIMA
Athens

Meaning "raw material" in Italian, Materia Prima was founded after sommelier Michalis Papatsimpas (*pictured on left*) travelled to Sicily, where he discovered natural wines and was inspired to open a wine bar. "It was named after the essence of the process, from the soil to the vines to the story of the land and relationships between people," says Papatsimpas. Materia Prima's first location opened in Koukaki in 2016, followed by another in Pangrati in 2019. Both feature artwork by calligrapher Greg Papagrigoriou and walk-in cellars where people can pick their bottles. "We want it to feel like selecting a record at a friend's house," says Papatsimpas.
materiaprima.gr

BAR
WINDMILL HYDRA
Hydra

BAR
180° SUNSET BAR
Mykonos

In Mykonos, lunchtime usually starts in the early afternoon and goes on until sunset. After that, any island devotee knows that a stopover at 180° Sunset Bar is the only way to keep up the momentum. The bar's beauty lies in its simplicity and bare interiors, which let the view of the whitewashed houses and port take centre stage. The drinks menu uses mostly Cycladic ingredients; we recommend the popular Serenity cocktail – blending aged *tsipouro* with coffee aromas – or Sentiment, a mix of mastiha, rose petals and mint. If you're after some light, pre-dinner bites, snacks like crunchy feta served with honey or watermelon carpaccio will do the trick. *180.bar*

Hydra's ancient windmill was immortalised in Sophia Loren's 1957 film *Boy on a Dolphin*. In 2023, it assumed a new purpose as the Windmill Hydra bar – the island's smallest watering hole. Liverpool-born Elaine Wong-Papoutsis and her Greek-Irish husband Jamie Papoutsis were captivated by the building's elevated position overlooking the splendid Saronic gulf. With such a supreme sunset view (the bar's opening hours work around Hydra's sunset times), the duo is low-key about their venture. "If people find us, then they find us, if they don't – then maybe next time they will," says Wong-Papoutsis. The Windmill's miniature lab concocts experimental cocktails incorporating ingredients as varied as soy sauce, cardamom and saffron. In the spirit of the island's banning of modern structures, each component of the bar blends in with Hydra's rustic landscape, from rattan umbrellas to the pebble-shaped speakers nestled into the stony verge on which the seats are perched.
Kanonia, Hydra 180 40

BAR

LOGGIA WINE BAR
Sifnos

BAR

SIMÁ
Tinos

Grab a table on the terrace at this bar on the outer rim of the citadel of Kastro, or perch directly on the white, cascading steps excavated into the rock. Founders Nikos Lavdas, Orestes Falireas and Nondas Pappas worked in the music industry before taking over this spot in 2021, so you can count on the soundtrack being just so. There are around 100 bottles on offer, but you're better off leaning into the casual atmosphere and asking for a glass of whatever's open in the chilled buckets on the serving counter; the team has also developed its own wine using assyrtiko grapes. In the kitchen, there's a revolving cast of chefs making tasty snacks.
Kastro, Sifnos

Though Ioanna Pilati's spot in the town of Pyrgos also serves small sharing plates based on her memories of traditional recipes, it's her commitment to championing independent winemakers that makes this an ideal spot for an aperitif. "Wine is what I love, and it's at the centre of Simá. We try to incorporate as many rare Greek varieties as possible," says Pilati (*pictured*) who opened this venture in 2022. Cycladian vineyards are invited to bring their wares to be sampled in Simá's breezy atmosphere. "When you walk in you should immediately feel you can relax," adds Pilati. It's easily done with a glass of rosé from Lemnos or a crisp white made in Epirus.
simatinos.com

BAR
YPSILON
Thessaloniki

In 2017, six friends decided that Thessaloniki was lacking a venue to host the city's burgeoning community of artists, creatives and startups. Ypsilon was the answer: a post-industrial, multifunctional space that can be divided to create just about any setup. The group rented the premises on the condition that they leave the building in its original state. True to their word, the exposed brick walls, wooden floorboards and steel columns of the 150-year-old building offer a rare insight into Thessaloniki's architecture before a fire destroyed much of the city in 1917. The airy interior hosts everything from exhibitions and concerts to art installations and workshops, and serves freddo espresso coffee and feta and tomato toasties until 20.00. But when the sun goes down, Ypsilon comes alive. That's when the glass doors slide open, the DJ sets begin and the hip crowd spills out of the building to party in the surrounding alleyways. "There's an open-minded community here and Ypsilon is at the heart of it," says co-founder Katerina Mamali. *ypsilon.com.gr*

ESTATE ARGYROS
Santorini

For millennia, Santorini's winemakers have been honing their methods to suit the island's lack of rain and scorching summers. Estate Argyros, founded in 1903, is the largest private owner of vineyards here, with holdings exceeding 120 hectares. "It's a unique wine zone," says Matthaios Argyros, the fourth-generation owner who's been at the helm since 2004. The soil on Santorini is famously volcanic but since it is very young it's difficult for vines to grow. There are benefits, however: a lack of potassium and clay gives it high acidity, making for a clean, crisp wine. Some 70 per cent of the grapes grown on Santorini are assyrtiko, an indigenous variety used to create lean, mineral whites celebrated since the days of ancient Greece. "Assyrtiko is a beautiful variety," says Argyros. "What fascinates me is its dynamic personality – how it can express itself so differently according to the winemaker's approach." Try the family's particularly refreshing version on a tour of the estate's minimalist headquarters, designed by local architects Oikos.
estateargyros.com

WINERY
PAPAGIANNAKOS
Mesogeia

Window-seat flyers coming into Athens International Airport are bound to notice one of the area's most important and ancient winemaking regions: Mesogeia. "Savatiano is our native grape, enjoyed during the time of Aristotle and Socrates," says Vassilis Papagiannakos (*pictured*) – third-generation winemaker at Papagiannakos estate – of the area's bright-gold, dry white grape. Though the winery was founded in 1919, it only officially started bottling and selling its savatiano under its own name in 1996. Today the vineyard exports 70 per cent of its splendid white wine.
papagiannakos.gr

Estate visits

Tours take place by appointment all year round at Papagiannakos estate. Architecture aficionados should make a point of stopping by the main building: the structure – the country's first bioclimatic winery – uses construction methods that reduce energy usage by 35 per cent. When it comes to tasting, the savatiano is obviously a must, but try the winery's retsina too.

35N
Sfakaki, Crete

On the outskirts of Rethymno, 35N distillery produces *tsikoudia*, a fiery spirit made using grape remnants from the winemaking process that has been enjoyed here since the start of the Ottoman occupation. In 2019 three friends turned co-founder Elias Melissourgos's distilling hobby into a brand, named after the line of latitude that runs through Crete. Today copper tanks are heated using steam made by burning olive pits, themselves waste products of the island's oil mills. Their *tsikoudia* – made with thyme mountain honey (courtesy of Cretan apiarists) – makes for a satisfying digestif after an indulgent *meze* feast.

35n.gr

METAXA LIKNON
Samos

For millennia, the mountain slopes on the island of Samos have produced the finest muscat grapes – the key ingredient in Metaxa, the iconic Greek spirit. This is where Metaxa Liknon has its roots. Liknon's award-winning visitor centre – opened to the public in 2022 and designed by Athens-based architects K-Studio *(see page 187)* – mirrors the vineyard terraces, with low-rise stepped buildings housing a bar and heritage centre. The island of Samos was the home of Epicurus, the Greek philosopher who held that the purpose of life was enjoyment: live up to his ideals with a glass of this sweet, sticky nectar.

metaxa.com

OLIVE OIL

DR KAVVADIA'S ORGANIC FARM
Corfu

On the road between the ancient ruins of Palaiokastritsa and Corfu old town, Dr Kavvadias's Organic Farm is an olive oil business with a personal approach. Owner Apostolos Porsanidis-Kavvadia (*pictured left*) has transformed his grandfather's old holiday home and outbuildings using his experience working at a design studio in Milan. Porsanidis-Kavvadia guides guests through the process: from harvesting and washing to milling and extracting the oil and tasting it directly from the machine. If you visit near harvest season, you can even make your own.
drkavvadia.com

Big oil
Olive oil manufacturing is big business in Greece: the country is the third-biggest producer in the world, with up to 390,000 tonnes of the liquid being made every year. Most of the largest olive farms are on Crete or on the Peloponnese peninsula.

FOOD RETAILER
DAPHNIS AND CHLOE
Athens

"The way I procure herbs is the same old-fashioned, person-to-person method my grandfather used to buy tobacco in the mountains," says Evangelia Koutsovoulou from the headquarters and shop of her brand Daphnis and Chloe at the foot of the Acropolis, where she also offers herb tastings. "You can smell Daphnis and Chloe all the way to the corner," she says. Koutsovoulou collects heirloom varieties from producers around Greece, including sesame seeds, Aegean oregano and lemon verbena. The enterprise takes her to the country's farthest corners to discover distinctive varieties, and the production process is age-old: wild herbs grow the way they always have and small-time farmers still gather, dry and cure them. "When people try our herbs, even if they don't know anything about cooking, they understand the difference in quality," says Koutsovoulou. "Plants in their natural habitat have no need for chemicals to help them thrive. Terroir is everything in winemaking but also in herbs."
daphnisandchloe.com

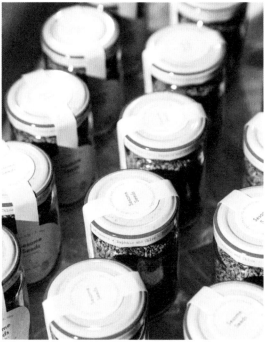

FOOD RETAILER
PALEO
Athens

This warehouse on gallery-lined Polidefkous Street in the port district of Piraeus was turned into a wine shop-bar-restaurant by sommelier Yiannis Kaimenakis (*pictured*) and has kept all of its raw, industrial edge. Spanish, Italian, and, most of all, Greek wines adorn the soaring walls: if you're unsure what to choose, Kaimenakis is always happy to weigh in. The extensive wine list spans around 300 labels, and you're welcome to try a glass among the stripped-back tables and school-like chairs, embossed with names of grape varieties. To eat, there are nibbles such as charcuterie and cheese boards, or more substantial plates from risotto to tartare.
Polidefkous 39, Athens

FOOD RETAILER
NERO
Spili, Crete

Before Athenian transplant Alexandra Alexopoulou opened this deli in the village of Spili in central Crete, the space was an "everything store" run by her father-in-law for nearly 60 years. Alexopoulou had been working at a shoe company but was looking for something different. Nero, meaning water in Greek and named after the village's many fountains, opened in 2022. "Greece is not just sea and sand, it's also about stories," says Alexopoulou. Each product, from olive oil to tea, chocolate and sea salt, is chosen partly for the narrative and integrity behind the brand. "I cannot sell something unless I have something to say about it," she explains.
+30 693 658 0419

YIAYIA AND FRIENDS
Thessaloniki

Not everyone's grandmother is a gatekeeper of wonderful recipes, but the founders of food firm Yiayia and Friends (*yiayia* meaning "grandma" in Greek) surely could count on theirs. The cheery brand pays homage to Greek matriarchs through its production of luxurious olive oil, balsamic vinegar, carrot breadsticks and cinnamon biscuits to furnish the larder. "Yiayias would never make it through a typical marketing process," says co-founder Konstantinos Poulopoulos of his decision to harness and package these recipes in a contemporary way. The brand's own design agency, Beetroot, came up with a playful depiction of an all-knowing Greek grandmother for the line's colourful packaging. In 2022, the company opened a food store in Thessaloniki next to the Beetroot HQ, in a residence rebuilt in 1926 after Thessaloniki's great fire. The brand's Greco-Levantine restaurant, Poster, is also next door. "The story, the visuals and the values are what matters for conscious consumers," says Poulopoulos. As for matters of taste, *yiayia* knows best.
yiayiaandfriends.com

FOOD RETAILER
ERGON AGORA
Thessaloniki

The foundations of Greece's food hall-cum-restaurant chain Ergon Agora are rooted in Thessaloniki. Thomas and George Douzis opened their flagship deli in their hometown in 2008. Since then, the brand has expanded: Ergon Agora East is set on an organic farm in Pylaia, 10km from the city centre. In a 1970s industrial shell, floor-to-ceiling windows overlook a vegetable garden and there's an on-site butcher, fishmonger, bakery and wine cellar. Elevated Greek fare on the menu includes chargrilled chicken gyros, slow cooked lamb with aubergine, harissa and yoghurt and filled *bougatsa* pastry. *ergonfoods.com*

MARKET
VARVAKIOS FISH MARKET
Athens

Varvakios Central Market is an Athenian institution. As well as trading in fruit and vegetables, nuts, dried goods and spices, the great atrium is home to the city's largest fish market. Supplying Athenians with their fill of the daily catch, as well as octopus, squid and other seafood, the fish market at Varvakios is a chaotic onslaught of the senses. Beyond the obvious olfactory overload, traders yell over the clamour, each offering a better price for their tuna steak or kilo of *sardeles* (sardines) and *gavro* (anchovies). It's not for the faint-hearted – but a great experience nonetheless.
Athinas 42, Athens

Open all eras
Known to locals as "the belly of Athens", Varvakios market has been operating since 1886. In that time, the market has survived earthquakes, bombings and a civil war, as well as plans to build a high-rise in its place during Greece's military dictatorship in the 1970s.

MARKET
EXARCHIA FARMERS' MARKET
Athens

Once known as the anarchist neighbourhood of Athens, Exarchia has changed dramatically in the last decade but retains some of its edgy character. Every Saturday at the base of the Kallidromiou steps, vendors line each side of the street under the shade of orange awnings, behind tables heaped with everything from olives to honey, tomatoes, peaches, onions, watermelons and crates of freshly caught fish. As one of the busiest markets in Athens, the atmosphere is cheerful, with families mixing with seniors, artists and students: testament to the area's strong community spirit.
Kallidromiou, Athens

DISCOVER GREECE | MARKETS

Greece has plenty of excellent ingredients to choose from when it comes to food and drink. Now a new generation are adapting those raw materials in delicious new ways. We talk to three leaders in the industry.

MEET THE EXPERTS

THANASIS PANOURGIAS
Bardót

Restaurateurs and co-owners Thanasis Panourgias (*pictured, centre*), Harry Spyrou (*right, with architect Andreas Kostopoulos*) and Leon Economidi opened cocktail bar Bardót in 2023. The trio also launched design gallery Maison Bardót (*see page 105*) nearby.

What was the inspiration behind Bardót?
The building itself has existed since the 1800s. It felt right to layer on a modern twist while maintaining its original quality. The walls on the patio and the materials used to build it are a true ode to the ancient Greek gods and the way everything was created. I was adamant about staying true to our Greek heritage.

How does the hospitality industry in Greece (and Antiparos) compare to other islands and countries around the world?
The hospitality industry in Greece, especially during summer, is at the highest level worldwide. I say that having lived and worked in New York for over 20 years.

What is your connection to the island?
It goes back 25 years, when I was spending all my summers in Mykonos. We had a friend in Antiparos with an amazing house and we'd come every summer. This island makes you travel back in time; that's the magic of the place. Antiparos is the best-kept secret. *Antíparos 840 07*

CHEF-OWNER
SOTIRIS KONTIZAS
Tanpopo

Greek-Japanese chef Sotiris Kontizas left a career in
a bank to pursue his passion for food. Thanks to his
appearances on Greek TV, he is a familiar face for many
in the country. His latest venture is Tanpopo, a ramen
joint in Athens, where he is executive chef and co-owner.

How does the industry in Athens compare to elsewhere?
I believe the hospitality industry in Athens is doing
great. Lots of new projects in cool neighbourhoods and
specialisation is blooming. For me, Athens is the place.

*How did you decide to combine Greek and Japanese flavours
in your cooking?*
I have a Greek father and a Japanese mother and I
was born and raised in Athens. My mother is a hell of
a cook. When she came here, she had to learn Greek
recipes with Greek ingredients but she didn't know
Greek techniques, only Japanese. So she improvised. It
was a fusing of the two and that's what I grew up with.

Do you think global influences are shaping Greek cuisine?
Yes, Greek cuisine is influenced by global trends. But
that's always been the case. People travel, cooks travel.
Everyone is influenced by everyone. Greek cuisine is
also influencing the world.

*Where did you get the idea to open up a Japanese restaurant
in Greece?*
First of all, Juzo Itami's 1985 movie *Tampopo* with
Ken Watanabe and Nobuko Miyamoto was a huge
inspiration. Then there's my love for soups, noodles
and vegetables. Tanpopo is a place where you can come
alone, slurp a bowl of ramen and be happy.
tanpopo.gr

WINEMAKER
ILIANA MALIHIN
Iliana Malihin Winery

Winemaker Iliana Malihin established her winery
on Mount Vouvala in 2019 after recognising the
undiscovered potential of the ancient vineyards of
Rethymno, Crete.

How does the terroir affect the taste of the wine?
Rethymno has a very nice microclimate because the
vines are at a high altitude of between 600 and 900m.
The schist soil contains sand and clay, which is unusual
for Crete, where the soil tends to be lime soil. We're also
close to the sea, which gives the wines a hint of salinity.

How would you describe the state of the Greek wine industry?
The Greek wine scene, and especially the Cretan one,
has risen in the last 15 years. This is because the next
generation of winemakers took over, and these people
had studied oenology and viticulture. They came into
winemaking with more knowledge and they made better
quality wines.

Why do you enjoy being a winemaker?
I couldn't think of being anything different. I enjoy
every single step and especially the work in the
vineyard. I like collaborating with my team, which
consists of many members of different ages and
mindsets. I love the process of taking a grape, turning it
into wine and communicating it to the world. Of course
I enjoy the "dirtiness" of this job – to get dirty with soil,
must and grapes and to feel free.
Melampes 740 53, Crete

From fashion to furniture and soap to flowers, entrepreneurs have tapped into ancient traditions to inspire their ventures. Keep an open mind and take an empty suitcase when you visit.

DESIGN & RETAIL

Greece's bounty of traditional craft is mirrored in a diverse range of products that often blend ancient techniques with modern sensibilities. For a taste of what a contemporary Greek fashion house can offer, look out for the elegant designs of Zeus & Dione, a brand renowned for its luxurious blend of classic Greek aesthetics and up-to-date style. In Athens, the Anthologist design shop offers an on-point selection of unique homewares that showcase the creative spirit of the nation. While you are in town, there's a plethora of retailers that warrant a visit: anything from old-school tailors to divine-smelling apothecaries and jewellers. Don't miss a visit to Ancient Greek Sandals where you'll find finely made footwear inspired by time-honoured designs. After years with a dormant economy, Greece is seeing a new generation of designers and retailers setting up colourful shops, not only in the capital, but from Thessaloniki to Tinos, Antiparos to Corfu. Let's go shopping.

THE EDIT

1 **Fashion**
Spots to refit your wardrobe with dresses, suits and sandals.

2 **Design**
Beautiful, striking and often surprising objects made by very smart creatives.

3 **Specialists**
From olive soap to fisherman's caps to handmade Cretan lyras: a list of artisans behind stunning products.

4 **Concept**
Three stores that have brought an artful approach to retail.

5 **The experts**
We meet some Greek entrepreneurs and learn their inspirations.

FASHION

MOUKI MOU
Athens

Nearly a decade after opening her pint-sized but influential London boutique Mouki Mou, Greek-born retailer Maria Lemos (*pictured left*) started imagining what an Athens iteration of the shop would look like – and in 2023 she found the right spot in the Plaka neighbourhood. On the shelves there's a handsome selection of homeware and womenswear, picked to reflect Lemos's slow-fashion ethos and penchant for textured pieces and imperfect shapes. "We want to have a point of view that fits the country. Greece is about simplicity and minimalism, and less is more," says Lemos.
moukimou.com

Smart home
The ambience of the store is important to Lemos. "The location felt so unique that the decision was instinctive," she says. She gave free rein to Thessaloniki-born designer Leda Athanasopoulou, who let the building's 1970s architecture define the shop's interiors, which feature repurposed terrazzo floors and aluminium and MDF accents.

DISCOVER GREECE | FASHION

FASHION
ZEUS & DIONE
Athens

Zeus & Dione is committed to creating
sleek, wearable designs that combine
heritage with a contemporary sensibility,
while revitilising traditional Greek
craftsmanship. Founded in 2013
by Dimitra Kolotoura and Mareva
Grabowski (*pictured*), their elegant
peplum dresses, plissé blouses and
roomy trousers all unmistakably nod
to motifs drawn from Greek antiquity.
Since launching its ready-to-wear
collection, the team has partnered with
artisans from jewellers to ceramicists for
their line, which has grown to include
accessories and homewares. Other than
the flagship store on Kolonaki's well-
heeled Voukourestiou Street, you'll find
a second outpost on the breezy Athenian
Riviera at the Vouliagmeni marina.
zeusndione.com

FASHION
IT'S A SHIRT
Athens

This fashion brand is a family affair: founder Christina Christodoulou (*pictured*) works with her father's tailoring workshop to create her shirt and jacket designs, which are sewn together a short drive from her shop in the neighbourhood of Exarchia. The company launched in 2017, when Christodoulou returned from four years in Sweden to start a label combining Scandinavian aesthetics and Greek manufacturing traditions. "We have a huge heritage in Greece regarding the textile industry," says Christodoulou, who sources fabrics from a family-run factory in Nafpaktos, as well as deadstock textiles from suppliers in Athens and poplins from Italy and Switzerland. Made of unusual cloth, the resulting garments feel surprising to the touch.
itsashirt.gr

FASHION
WAIKIKI
Andros

In the neoclassical capital of Andros, the northernmost island in the Cyclades, Kiki Senteli puts together a collection of wares – some her own designs, others from up-and-coming artisans and well-known brands – in her matchbox-sized lifestyle shop. She turns to her Greek heritage for inspiration, looking closely at the styles her mother and grandmother wore. The rails contain long flowing dresses, while in the windows there are straw bags and slip-on shoes for the summer. On the island, she also likes to work with other creators. Her latest line of kitchen essentials is a collaboration with an island neighbour: creative guesthouse Mèlisses (*see page 17*).
Andros 845 00

FASHION
KOUTSIKOU
Hydra

Being so close to Athens means that the island of Hydra benefits from a cosmopolitan flair in retail matters. Originally opened on the island of Kythira in 2018 by Lea Paolini, her mother Maria and her husband Walter (an expert in fine Italian design), the shop opened in a second space opposite Hydra's port in 2019. Today, it sells Italian design staples – flowery blouses and skirts, colour-popping sandal and striped shirts – as well as crochet shoes by Kashura, Indonesia-made hats by Lorna Murray and jewellery by Greek designer Katerina Chatzipetraki. The mother-daughter duo also started their own homewares line, Casa Koutsikou, in 2024.
koutsikou.com

FASHION
PARTHENIS
Mykonos

Orsalia Parthenis grew up immersed in the eponymous fashion brand started by her father, designer Dimitris Parthenis and has been leading the brand since 1996. The elder Parthenis opened his first shop in Athens in 1970, and followed it up eight years later with a boutique on Mykonos. The island has served as a constant source of inspiration even as the label achieved broader renown, with six boutiques across Greece and a worldwide wholesale network. "Mykonos is awash with Cycladic light, which is unique in its contrast and shadow," says Orsalia. "It's also an island that's alive 24/7." That sense of dynamism is key to Parthenis's approach to design, with its clothing made of all-natural linens, cottons, wools and silks. Most items embody what the family calls a "chic sportif" spirit and a relaxed but confident air. "The clothes are glamorous and at the same time bohemian," says Parthenis. "They do not discriminate by size or sex, and they are easy to care for and pack to go onto the next adventure."
orsalia-parthenis.gr

FASHION
AESTHET
Mykonos

Multi-brand boutique Aesthet hosts a number of Greek labels under one roof, from Zeus & Dione to summer specialist Ancient Kallos and jewellers Lito and Ileana Makri (*see page 100*). "We were the first boutique to bring together local designers in about 2013," says founder Alexandra Zakka. "Before that we were governed by xenocentrism and everything was imported." Building on the success of her flagship store in the Kolonaki district of Athens, Zakka has opened a second on Mykonos and is planning another in the new Ellinikon Mall in Athens. "There's ongoing demand from both tourists and locals," she says.
aesthet.com

FASHION
PARA TODOS
Thessaloniki

As its name implies (*para todos* means "for all" in Spanish), the clean, simple lines and oversized shapes of this label's collections are designed for everyone. Founded by brother and sister Tassos Tsadaris and Christina Tsadari (*pictured*), the company focuses on clothing made from natural fabrics, cut and sewn by hand. "We're strict on this," says Tsadari. "We don't use synthetic materials and choose environmentally friendly cottons, wools and linens." Thanks to smart, tailored finishes and neat pleating, there's a refined edge to this casual line – as well as a hint of streetwear and Asian inspiration to its kimono shirts and balloon trousers.
paratodos.gr

FASHION
MAISON STAMATA
Tinos

Maison Stamata opened in 2023 in Tinos town to bring a dose of French resort wear to the Greek island. The shop was opened by Helene de Garder (*pictured*), who looked to her great-grandmother's love for local tradition and appreciation of beautiful objects for inspiration. In among this nostalgic mix of pool floats, striped towels and brightly coloured one-piece swimsuits, there's also easy linen shirts, capacious beach bags, shady straw hats and minimalist leather sandals. Decked out across the walls are gilt religious motifs, reflecting the iconography the island is famous for.
Gizi 7, Tinos

The house on the hill
Helene de Garder's great-grandmother did not just inspire Maison Stamata's contents. The shop is named after her 19th-century home in the hilltop village of Pyrgos: *stamata* means "stop" in Greek.

MENSWEAR
CHRISTAKIS
Athens

Christos Nyflis helps run the exquisite menswear shop founded by his grandfather – the titular Christakis – in 1947. "He came to Athens from what was then Constantinople in 1934," says Nyflis. "After some years, he managed to open his own store." Friendly service and the artisanal techniques used in the workshop are key to their success. "We developed a unique approach to translating body measurements into personalised patterns," he says. "We believe cutting is as crucial as sewing, which is why it is all done by hand, letting us incorporate a bit of our soul into each garment."
christakisathens.com

Buttoned-up family
Christos's mother Vicky and brother Antonis work alongside him at Christakis, maintaining the family legacy by making bespoke shirts, overshirts and loungewear, using high-quality materials such as ultrafine cotton poplin. The process requires skill and precision, with certain details, such as button and monogram sewing, carried out entirely by hand.

MENSWEAR
MOHXA
Athens

MENSWEAR
NÉ EN AOÛT
Mykonos

Its name may mean "born in August" in French, but Né en Août is a proudly Mykonian retailer. This menswear label embraces a minimal aesthetic, using natural materials like linen and organic cotton for its sleek, simple silhouettes. Inspired by French and Japanese fashion, the brand's elegant staples come in boxy fits elevated by surprising pleated details at the sleeves, or pin tucks on the trousers. No island-based label would be complete without swimwear: Né en Août's collection of swim shorts have become easily recognisable thanks to their colourful patterns, featuring palm trees to dolphins in their cheerful, graphic prints.
neenaout.com

Mohxa's surf-inspired retro tees, caps, totes and trousers are the fruit of a childhood friendship. George Papachatzopoulos and Iason Pachos (*pictured*) conceived of the brand in 2013 after reuniting in the Greek capital. "After half an hour of talking we headed off to buy fabrics," says Pachos. "We decided to take them and make new clothes." Plenty lay waiting to be found: Greece's textile industry was booming in the 1990s until new regulations slashed exports and left warehouses full of deadstock. The pair now operate out of their Athens store. "We want to offer a total collection that goes beyond just clothes," says Papachatzopoulos.
mohxa.com

JEWELLERY
ILEANA MAKRI
Athens

Ileana Makri's fortunes as a jeweller took off when Barneys New York fell in love with her classic thread ring design – an infinity band of fine diamonds – and since then, the Greece-based designer has turned to her travels around the world for inspiration, not strictly sticking to any single theme for each successive collection. In her Athens atelier, her steady-handed team works with raw materials including enamel and gold, melding metals and stones in motifs of snakes, mosaic tiles (something she adores from her island home of Patmos) and celestial symbols.

ileanamakri.com

Jewel purpose

As a child growing up in Greece, Makri (*pictured below, on the right*) was fascinated by jewellery – so she made her own out of glass beads, lace and stones. As a teenager she would watch goldsmiths in Athens jewellery workshops to learn their techniques. In 1996 she decided to study jewellery design at the Gemological Institute of America in Santa Monica and started to craft her first proper designs.

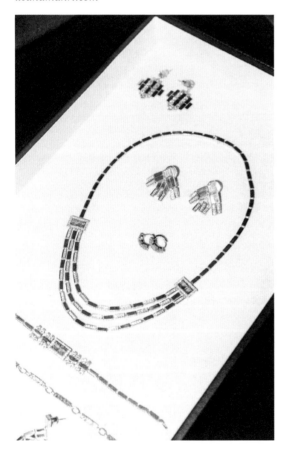

JEWELLERY
YANNIS SERGAKIS
Paros

SHOES
ANCIENT GREEK SANDALS
Athens

Ancient Greek Sandals began with a meeting between designer Christina Martini and Nikolas Minoglou, who comes from a family of shoemakers. Though the classic fisherman's sandal design with thin interlaced leather straps had always been popular, it was difficult to find any that balanced quality with affordability. "We felt there was a hole in the market: you could only find them at high-end shops or tourist kiosks," says Martini, whose husband, Apostolos Porsanidis-Kavvadia, runs Dr Kavvadia's Organic Farm on the island of Corfu (*see page 81*). Production began in 2012; each shoe is handmade locally using chemical-free tanned leather. The range keeps expanding and includes anything from sturdy slip-ons to flip-flops and gladiator models. Each is adorned with the brand's signature wing-shaped buckle – a homage to Hermes, the messenger god who famously wore winged shoes. If you can't visit the Athens store, there is another at the city's airport – so you can grab a pair before flying off yourself. *ancient-greek-sandals.com*

Athenian designer Yannis Sergakis (*pictured*) grew up in a family of jewellery traders and has followed in their footsteps. His signature line was launched in 2014 after almost a decade of refining his craft. Sergakis' jewels are handmade in his Athens workshop by artisans following longstanding techniques, though you'll also find them at the brand's Paros shop. "The atmosphere is as familiar as it is unique. It makes me feel connected to tradition while grounded in today's world," says Sergakis. His earrings, rings, bracelets and pendants are often studded with small diamonds arranged in geometric clusters, with a pleasingly contemporary sensibility. *yannissergakis.com*

DESIGN
OBJECTS OF COMMON INTEREST
Athens

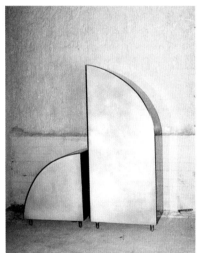

Duo Eleni Petaloti and Leonidas Trampoukis (*pictured*)
founded Objects of Common Interest in 2016 to explore
the intersection of art, design and architecture. Their
work spans furniture to immersive installations, with
a particular penchant for opalescent resin tables and
chairs. The studio's operations are split between
artisans working in Greece and logistics being handled
in New York. "Our Athens studio is the creative hub
where we test new materials and ideas – it's a sacred
place," says Petaloti. "No matter who we are working
with it's important to have a nod to Greece, whether
that's Athenian architecture or Cycladic island craft."
objectsofcommoninterest.com

DESIGN
YIANNIS GHIKAS
Athens

The road from computer science teacher to product designer is not often travelled. Yet in his early thirties, Yiannis Ghikas (*pictured*) decided he wanted a career change, so he retrained and began working late into the night. One of Ghikas' most renowned works was also the first to go into mass production: the Monarchy Stool, a four-legged wooden rocking stool. More recent work includes curvaceous glass Soda tables, and he has been collaborating with design store Myran on a range of ceramic mugs and bowls named "Artificiel" that plays on the idea of the city's skin: the textured façade applied to most Athenian buildings built between 1950 and 1970. *yiannisghikas.com*

DESIGN
PARAPHERNALIA
Athens

Angela Koutroulaki and George Karras started their shop in 2014 to fill the gap they perceived in Athens' design offering. "We wanted to create a place where people would feel welcome to chat and browse in a relaxed way, while also presenting a clear and unique aesthetic," says Koutroulaki. That's anything from candle-holders to roomy tables by international brands such as String and Ferm – as well as comely mid-century armchairs from Poland. The joyful jumble on display on the industrial-style shelves is aptly represented by the shop's name. "It's all pieces we truly liked, from nice pencils to larger furniture," adds Koutroulaki. *paraphernalia.gr*

DESIGN
ANTHOLOGIST
Athens

In Athens' central Vathis neighbourhood, US-born Andria Mitsakos (*pictured*) took over a neoclassical building and transformed it into a by-appointment *wunderkammer*. Her elegant emporium is brimming with items produced in workshops in Athens, Egypt and Armenia. "I have most of my bags, belts, ceramics, jewellery, furniture and stained glass made in this country. The remainder is a mix of items I source from my travels, one-off finds and antiques," she says. "Anthologist is a brand for collectors and those who want to surround themselves with beautiful craft."
anthologist.com

Art and soul
Through her business, Mitsakos is connecting the plethora of skilled artisans across the city with a new European and American clientele, who often come in to commission custom pieces. "There's a shift in perspectives and people's value systems so they're appreciating tradition again – what's old is new," she says. "People don't want cookie-cutter, they want pieces with history and soul."

DESIGN
MAISON BARDÓT
Antiparos

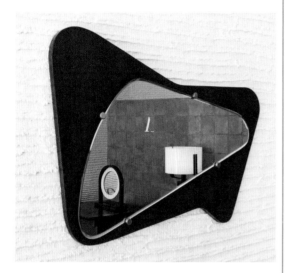

When Bardót – a grotto-like, ceramics-filled cocktail bar – opened on Antiparos in summer 2023, it was a smart and low-key addition to the island (*see page 88*). Now, New York design studio Manhattan Projects have paired up again with owner Thanasis Panourgias and restaurateur Harry Spyrou to launch the only design gallery on the island: Maison Bardót. Inside this former ice cream shop, Cycladic minimalism meets mid-century nostalgia, with rippled white-stucco walls and terracotta floor tiles. The idea is to mix local crafts with international interior pieces and to spark conversations about artisanship, architecture and aesthetics.
Pounta, Antiparos, 840 07

DESIGN
MORETHANTHIS
Antiparos

Design shop Morethanthis began life in 2014 as the office of interior designer Elena Xanthopoulou. From her luminous workplace in the heart of Antiparos town, she began selling jewellery and furnishings and over the years the studio gradually transformed into a dedicated retail space. "Initially, the shop was a way of keeping the items on display around me as I worked," says Xanthopoulou. Today, Morethanthis stocks predominantly Greek jewellery makers, including Athenian brands such as Myrto Anastasopoulou, Ioanna Souflia and Lito, as well as some European names including French jewellery designer Marie Lichtenberg and Belgian creative Celine Daoust. Morethanthis also sells contemporary furniture, ceramics and artworks, with sculptural marble lamps designed by Xanthopoulou herself, candlesticks, prints by Cyprus-born artist Philippos Theodorides and stoneware candlesticks, vases and plates by Athens-based Anna Karountzou and Ismene King.
morethanthis.gr

MOTIF
Syros

In 2022, former fashion editor Sandy Karagianni traded the bustle of Athens for the relaxed pace of island life on Syros. In these new sunny premises, she opened homeware shop Motif with her husband, Pericles. Here, the pair sell hand-crafted pieces, including ceramics from the island of Serifos and tiles inspired by the vernacular of the Cyclades. Although the homeware evokes historical Mediterranean heritage, most of the simple pieces have a modern sensibility that emphasises the use of natural materials. "We love the mixture of traditional and updated pieces," explains Karagianni. *motifdesign.gr*

Syros business
The relaxed atmosphere of her new island home is a vital part of the appeal for Karagianni. "We first came to Syros when we were invited by friends to stay at their home here," she says. "We immediately fell in love with the town and the beauty of its architecture."

DESIGN
TAXIDI
Tinos

Taking its name from the Greek word for "journey", Taxidi is the brainchild of Franco-Belgian creative director Virginie Muys (*pictured*) and Tinos native Manthos Kaloumenos. In 2021, the couple set about restoring a derelict 1930s property in the heart of Tinos town, which they opened a year later as a shop-cum-gallery. At its centre, a sun-dappled courtyard doubles as a café where visitors can enjoy coffee from Athenian roastery Kudu and food made using produce grown on the island. Inside, the shop stocks clothing, accessories and homeware, mostly from small Greek brands and makers such as Athenian jewellers Neso Studio and Vasiliki Studio, while the gallery is also filled with largely homegrown talent. *taxiditinos.com*

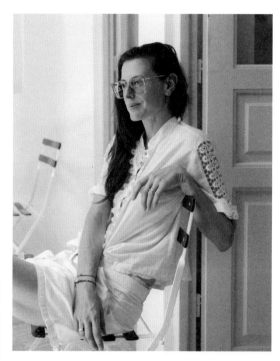

SPECIALIST
KOPRIA
Athens

Exuberant flower shop Kopria opened in 2018 on a quiet corner in Athens' edgy Exarchia neighbourhood. With its sky-blue door frame and mass of verdant leaves spilling out onto the pavement, it stocks plants of all sizes for both indoors and outdoors – from cacti to *monstera* to *ficus elastica*. Inside, you'll find bunches of fresh-cut flowers on sale, alongside design magazines, Japanese gardening tools and homewares crafted in Greece. The store also provides a decoration service for events as well as plant maintenance for homes, hotels and businesses.
Eresou 30, Athens

Blooming relationship
When photographer Ifigeneia Filipoulou and her partner Vasilis Nzeremes wrote down their dream jobs over coffee one morning and showed each other, they both landed on the same thing: "own a flower shop". "When I travelled I would take lots of pictures and eventually I realised they were always of plants in flower shops," says Filipoulou. "From that day on, we started looking for a space."

SPECIALIST
NAXOS APOTHECARY
Athens

Formerly known as Korres Pharmacy, the Naxos Apothecary has been providing Greeks with everything from homoeopathic remedies to luxury skincare products for over 30 years. The brand's Athens outpost pays homage to its namesake island – birthplace of founders Yorgos and Andonis Korres – with soaps, scents and salves made from Cycladic herbs. With white walls and warm wooden accents, the interiors have the feel of an old-school pharmacy, with amber bottles, fragrance-filled vials and a long counter for consultations. At the back, chemists in the open laboratory create bespoke potions tailored to individual needs.
thenaxosapothecary.com

SPECIALIST
CALLISTA
Athens

Celia Sigalou and Eleni Konstantinidou started Callista with grand ambitions: they wanted to create the perfect bag. As interest grew, the two women focused on championing Greek craftsmanship and empowering local women in the aftermath of the financial crisis. In 2016, the brand's flagship store opened on Voukourestiou Street. Today, the bags are handmade in Athens and feature crocheted and woven handles, using leather cord in consecutive knots and decoratively stitched seams. With such identifying details, Callista has no need for a logo: its designs have become a recognisable symbol of quality and ethical craftsmanship in themselves.
callista.com

SAVAPILE
Athens

Savapile's handmade straw hats have adorned heads in Athens since 1960. The brand has grown from humble origins, with founder Savvas Sarigiannidis starting out using pots and pans for moulds. "I learned the art from my father," says Lisa Sarigiannidou, who took over the business in 2011. Today, this is the last hat-making company in Athens to use the traditional handmade millinery technique. Sarigiannidou sells her custom-made creations wholesale to shops around the city, as well as exporting naval-style hats to the US and offering a bespoke service direct to customers from her millinery studio down a small side-street in the neighbourhood of Psyrri. Though mostly famous for its straw hats, Savapile is also known for its "fisherman's cap", derived from the style of traditional headgear worn by Greek seamen in the 19th century. Constructed by hand using a fine wool blend, each cap features an embroidered band across the brim and a plaited loop chain held down with matt anchor studs.

Agias Eleousis 14, Athens

SPECIALIST
OLGIANNA MELISSINOS SANDALS
Athens

The Athens neighbourhoods of Monastiraki and Plaka are home to family-run shops that have been turning out meticulously crafted items for generations. Olgianna Melissinos Sandals is one such spot. It offers some of the best made-to-measure leather sandals, made by owner Olgianna Melissinos (*pictured*), who is following in her father's footsteps. "I was scared of living up to his name; he had a reputation as a sandal-maker but also a poet," says Melissinos. She is always on hand to take customers' measurements and offer recommendations. "The concept of 'handmade' can be quite elitist but I want to make sure it is as accessible as possible," she says.
melissinos-sandals.gr

SPECIALIST
PATOUNIS SOAP
Corfu

"We have been producing traditional green olive soap since 1850. The main difference between this and the industrial version is that no additives are used," says Patounis' fifth-generation owner Apostolos Patounis (*pictured*), who chose to carry on this family business rather than pursue a career as an engineer. Together with a team of up to seven, depending on workload, Apostolos manufactures 18 tonnes of soap per year. The factory and adjoining shop, located in an inconspicuous one-storey building not far from the university in Corfu Town, resemble a museum: customers can get a peek into the elaborate production process here too.
patounis.gr

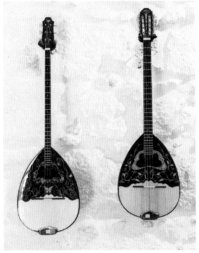

STAGAKIS CRETAN LYRA
Rethymno, Crete

The Cretan lyra is a pear-shaped bowed instrument native to the island that has also shaped the musical identity of other spots in the Aegean archipelago and the Dodecanese. In the 1940s, musician Manolis Stagakis decided that none of the lyras he was playing met his standards, so he decided to make his own. He set up a workshop in Rethymno and today the tradition continues with his grandson, Manolis Stagakis Jr (*pictured*). Ornate handmade instruments hang from the walls of the shop, ranging from the traditional Cretan lyra to elaborate mandolins and lutes.
stagakis-manolis.gr

In-store recital
Stagakis Jr can usually be found occupied in the open workshop at the back of his shop, but he will happily pull down one of his products to demonstrate its sound and tell the object's story: many of them are shaped from reclaimed wood from old buildings in the area.

CERAMICS
CHIMERA
Syros

In 2020, Manos Mastorakis gave up his corporate job to open ceramics shop and gallery Chimera in Ermoupolis. "Everything we stock is made in Greece," says Mastorakis, whose mother was born on Syros. Mastorakis commissioned architect Spiros Kapis to design the interior, where large windows and bright, whitewashed walls accentuate the pieces on display, ranging from porcelain bowls painted in brilliant red patterns to modernist-looking teapots adorned with cobalt and limestone strokes. The workshop also accommodates artist residencies and classes, giving visitors the chance to try out traditional Greek crafts. *chimeracraft.gr*

CERAMICS
MYRTO ZIRINI
CERAMICS
Corfu

Ceramicist Myrto Zirini (*pictured*) gave up a career in architecture in Athens to move to Corfu, where she established a workshop in 2017. "I spent summers here with my grandparents," she says. "Many creative people have made the same move, resulting in a community of passionate contemporary artists." Zirini's studio occupies a compact space in Corfu's old town. Inside, delicate vessels with organic, fluid forms and colourful glazed interiors line the shelves. Each piece is inspired by hues of the Ionian landscape. "I like to think of each piece as a cultural fossil," she says. "A unique shape that carries with it the specific characteristics of its location." *myrtozirini.gr*

CONCEPT STORE
APHILO
Athens

Harilaos Kourtinos Pallas opened Aphilo to provide a home for the city's up-and-coming artisans. The boutique brings together jewellers using upcycled materials, designers experimenting with natural dyeing techniques and self-taught ceramicists with the founder's own work, ranging from furniture to handcrafted garments. "We want to highlight skills being revived by young Athenians," says Pallas. His own brand, Kyr Lakis, is a homage to his grandfather's skill in traditional block printing. You can get his grandfather's drawings on elegant cotton shirts, silk scarves and canvas tote bags.
aphiloathens.com

CONCEPT STORE
PHAON
Athens

After living in Italy, where they worked in fashion and advertising, Dimitra Louana Marlanti and Alexandros Kalogiros (*pictured*) found themselves back in Athens during the pandemic. They decided to open a scent-related shop where they could stock products they had grown accustomed to abroad. Besides fragrances by international brands from Perfumer H to Ormaie and Santa Maria Novella, their offering also includes soap, vases, candles, incense and fresh bouquets. "Flowers do not only complement our fragrances but also embody a deeper symbolic meaning, especially in the act of giving, which is an aspect we want to emphasise," says Marlanti. *phaon-athens.com*

CONCEPT STORE
ZOSMA
Tinos

Gallery-boutique Zosma was set up in 2022 in what used to be the candle-making atelier of an orthodox priest. "We put together our painting-like votives and brooches using metal *támata* (ex-votos) and vintage textiles such as precious silks and velvets, as well as trims made with the Benaki Museum using their 19th-century looms," says co-founder Theodor Anastasato (*pictured*). The business also works with prolific mills that produce rich brocades used in the orthodox church – though for summer, there are roomy linen ensembles, breezy trousers in broderie anglaise and silk foulards.
Leof. Megalocharis 31, Tinos

Pilgrims and progress
Tinos has been a destination for religious pilgrims since antiquity, but the island has developed rapidly in the past few years. Zosma co-founders Theodor Anastasato and Patricia Fernandez-Navarro chose the shop's name as a reference to the old custom of measuring the diameter of a temple with a cord, an image that encapsulates the inspiration they draw from both Hellenic craft and religion.

Greece has a craft history reaching back thousands of years, but these traditions are being brought up to date by a new crop of modern practitioners. We talk to three of them.

MEET THE EXPERTS

RETAILER

EVA PAPADAKI
10AM Apotheke

10AM Apotheke founder Eva Papadaki sought to celebrate the landscapes of Crete and the talent of the island's artisans in her homeware and skincare brand, which she runs from multi-purpose space 10AM Lofts in downtown Athens. Other than selling soaps, tea and candles, she bottles oil and thyme honey from Rethymno and has her own line of deliberately misshapen ceramics.

What is your brand's philosophy?
10AM Apotheke is centred around a return to simplicity and a respect for nature. We celebrate the small, everyday joys that come from reconnecting with our roots, and supporting independent producers.

How does Crete inspire you?
I have a deep connection to Crete, where everything was handmade. I created the brand to celebrate these traditions and to introduce others to the essence of a life lived in harmony with the landscape.

How are your products made?
We follow age-old methods passed down through generations and use sustainable materials like home-grown herbs, honey, olive oil, and sea salt. We work closely with small producers who share our dedication and who respect the rhythms of nature.
10amapotheke.com

DESIGNER
ELINA TSELIAGKOU
Unsung Weavers

When Elina Tseliagkou relocated from London back to her hometown of Athens in 2017, she came across some traditional Greek handwoven wool blankets. Taken by their special texture and their particular craftsmanship, she started a business salvaging these precious textiles and turning them into one-of-a-kind garments.

What is your brand's ethos?
I would describe it as an alternative model of made-to-order customised garments – in opposition to the fast-fashion model. We favour singularity instead of bigger automated production and we honour the irregularities in the handmade processes.

Why Athens?
There is a great dynamism in the city of Athens. On one hand there are a lot of creatives from abroad operating here and staying for different periods of time. But there's also an older generation of Greeks who are knowledgeable about traditional crafts and are very willing to share it. I love bridging and reshuffling these two distant realities

How has the Greek fashion scene evolved?
Greek fashion was sealed off and outdated, with a particular idea of luxury in mind. Now I am happy to see the industry embracing new silhouettes and seeking inspiration from a wider pool of Greek cultural references that sometimes originate from modern Greece, not just the glorified, ancient past.
unsungweavers.com

DESIGNER
MARILENA ANDREADI
Maan Swimwear

Marilena Andreadi founded her swimwear brand Maan in 2014; her environmentally conscious, elegant line is meant to echo the slow lifestyle of the Greek islands and has been making a splash in fashion boutiques since.

What is Maan's ethos?
Our collections are all about being smart and effortlessly stylish, with a focus on sustainability and top-notch quality, minus the fuss.

What are your inspirations?
We're continually captivated by the raw Cycladic beauty, with our prints reflecting the untamed allure of the Greek landscape. Our colour palette channels the essence of the Greek islands – imagine hidden beaches where turquoise waters meet golden sands, dramatic limestone cliffs soaring into the sky, and rusty-red sea rocks where rare birds find sanctuary.

Maan is designed in Antiparos and sold in Athens, what do you love most about these two places?
Antiparos is a place where I can stand still and breathe. Blending in with the locals there has been life-changing, and it's at the heart of Maan's essence. On the other hand, our Athens showroom is the brand's creative base. It's where everything happens; where every aspect of production comes together.
maanislandwear.com

We've compiled a round-up of our favourite Greek products to help
you pick out the perfect souvenir – from handmade leather
sandals to beautiful ceramics from the islands.

THE SHOPPING LIST

1 Yiayia and Friends chilli olive oil
yiayiaandfriends.com
2 Agrifarm giant beans
agrifarm.gr
3 Ancient Greek Sandals, Maria sandals
ancient-greek-sandals.com
4 Traditional textiles
Widely available
5 Daphne Leon Greek salad ceramics
daphneleon.com
6 Korres *halvadopita* (halva pie)
agorafoodtrading.com
7 Chios *mastiha* gum
Widely available
8 Andromache milk and dark chocolate
andromache.gr

1 Darema orange cookies
  Widely available
2 Museum of Cycladic Art ceramic plate
  cycladic.gr
3 Helleo olive oil soap
  helleo.gr
4 Cushion covers from Anthologist
  anthologist.com
5 Mesklies nougat bar
  mesklies.gr
6 Varsos nut bar
  varsos.gr
7 Daphnis and Chloe smoked chilli flakes
  daphnisandchloe.com
8 Kalaman heather honey
  +30 699 686 3880

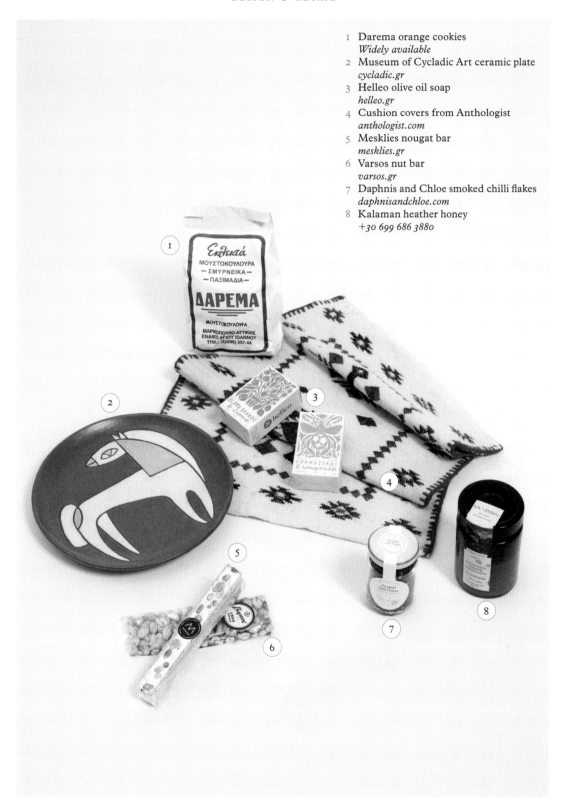

1 Rafalias Pharmacy almond oil
 rafalias.com
2 Physis Laboratory beeswax cream
 physislaboratory.com
3 Mythos beer
 Widely available
4 Alfa Hellenic beer
 Widely available
5 Nimos visor by Blanc
 blanc.gr
6 Maan Island bikini
 maanislandwear.com
7 Milk White sunglasses
 milkwhite.gr

1   Naxos Apothecary facial toner, eau de
    parfum and soap
    thenaxosapothecary.com
2   Zeus & Dione Thalassini bag
    zeusndione.com
3   *Doors of Kypseli* book by Eleanor Lines,
    published by Hyper Hypo
    eleanorlines.com; hyperhypo.gr
4   Silver rings by Swim to the Moon
    swimtothemoonjewelry.com
    Diamond-studded gold rings by
    Yannis Sergakis
    yannissergakis.com; moukimou.com

Opal beaded necklace by Ileana Makri
ileanamakri.com; moukimou.com
Diamond-studded gold band ring and
diamond bead ring by Fanourakis
fanourakis.gr; moukimou.com
5   DK Ceramics blue flowers plate
    +30 693 443 3453
6   Eye rings and earring by Leda
    Athanasopoulou
    ledaathanasopoulou.com; moukimou.com
7   Naxos Apothecary body balm
    thenaxosapothecary.com

1 Physis Laboratory foam bath,
  shampoo and conditioner
  physislaboratory.com
2 Ktima Kir-Yianni Tarsanas assyrtiko
  white wine 2022
  kiryianni.gr
3 It's A Shirt anthracite shirt
  itsashirt.gr
4 Ancient Greek Sandals, Bios sandals
  ancient-greek-sandals.com
5 Ergon Aegean sardines
  ergonfoods.com
6 Yiayia and Friends balsamic vinegar
  yiayiaandfriends.com

1 Museum of Cycladic Art ceramic jug
   cycladic.gr
2 Ceramic bird by Keramika Kostas
   Depastas, Sifnos
   Cheronissos Bay, Sifnos
3 Fix Hellas beer
   Widely available
4 Haraki Cretan tsikoudia
   Widely available
5 Nikos Haristakis hand-blown
   champagne and wine glass
   moukimou.com

6 Trela Scents of Tinos ouzo candle
   trelatinos.com
7 Deneké extra virgin olive oil
   Widely available
8 Isidoros Arvanitis ouzo of Plomari
   ouzoplomari.gr
9 Manousos ceramic pomegranate
   moukimou.com
10 Thalia-Maria Georgoulis silver spoons
   moukimou.com

1   Dyo Ipsi Estate Dialogos kydonitsa &
    assyrtiko white wine 2023
    dioipsi.com
2   Ergon infused olive oil selection
    ergonfoods.com
3   Brass coffee pot
    Widely available
4   Salt Odyssey sea salt flakes
    saltodyssey.com
5   Brass Arion dolphin from Anthologist
    anthologist.com
6   Manopoulos backgammon board game
    manopoulos.com

1 Kayafas xinomavro naoussa 2018
  red wine
  thymiopoulosvineyards.gr
2 Hak Studios red leather tote bag
  hak-studios.com
3 Daphnis and Chloe recovery herbal
  and mountain tea
  daphnisandchloe.com
4 DK Ceramics red flowers plate
  +30 693 443 3453
5 Pitsiladi ouzo
  Widely available
6 Caprice chocolate crispy wafers
  papadopoulou.gr
7 Iliana Malihin vidiano and
  thrapsathiri Lefkós white wine
  +30 697 934 4044
8 Ergon Aegean sea salt
  ergonfoods.com

As the birthplace of European civilisation, Greece is brimming with culture. This is our list of places where you can experience that remarkable heritage, as well as the thrilling art being created now.

CULTURE

With an ancient heritage that has influenced and inspired thinkers, poets and artists for millennia, Greece also has plenty to offer today. The Acropolis still watches over Athens and the city's pulse can be felt in its many world-class museums and galleries. The National Museum of Contemporary Art leads the way in terms of cutting-edge exhibitions, while the Goulandris Museum of Contemporary Art is the place to admire modern masterpieces. Many islands are home to a bohemian cohort of creatives seeking inspiration in the elemental landscape – and now have the venues to prove it. Thessaloniki also comes alive with its acclaimed festivals, which bring anything from indie film screenings to jazz nights to the northern city. Traditional music and theatre continue to evolve, blending old and new in amphitheatres and modern institutions alike. Still, you can't leave without visiting an archaeological museum or two – to truly feel the power of history.

THE EDIT

1 Museums
The best of the nation's historical repositories.

2 Galleries
Spaces championing Greece's thriving art scene.

3 Art venues
Multi-disciplinary spots playing host to a variety of events.

4 Record shops & music venues
For enthusiasts who like their music in a tangible form; and listening in charming surroundings.

5 Open-air cinemas
A much-beloved and still hugely popular Greek tradition.

6 Bookshops
Attractive and dynamic shops dedicated to the printed word.

7 The experts
Three cultural leaders give us their thoughts on Greece's arts scene.

MUSEUM
NATIONAL ARCHAEOLOGICAL MUSEUM
Athens

There is no shortage of archaeological museums around Greece – virtually every island or region has its own – but if you can only visit one, make it this. The National Archaeological Museum houses one of the most important ancient art collections in the world, perhaps rivalled only by its counterparts in Naples and Cairo. Built between 1866 and 1889, the neoclassical building in Exarchia is the repository of over 16,000 sculptures from sites across the country. The collection covers over 7,000 years of history, leading visitors from prehistoric clay figurines to bronze and marble masterpieces from the height of classical antiquity. Though its holdings have always been spectacular, the building has long needed improvement. This is set to change with a renovation by British architect David Chipperfield, who is planning a raised public garden with 20,000 sq m of gallery space below. The expansion is welcome, since 90 per cent of the collection is in storage. Construction is expected to last five years but the start date is yet to be determined.
namuseum.gr

MUSEUM
NATIONAL MUSEUM OF CONTEMPORARY ART
Athens

If you're looking for a modern take on Greece's cultural scene, take a short walk from the Acropolis to the National Museum of Contemporary Art (EMST for short) in the city's buzzing Koukaki district. Housed in a building that once contained Greece's oldest brewery, the enormous space is used as a pared-back setting for EMST's cutting-edge collection. Founded in 1997, the institution celebrates Greek visual culture in all its forms, as well as collaborating with international artists. Dip in to take part in performance and interactive events – in the summer, the museum also hosts an open-air cinema. After you're done, head to the rooftop where EMST's gourmet restaurant Nyn Esti serves dishes from turbot and cockles to wild boar. *emst.gr*

MUSEUM

MUSEUM OF CYCLADIC ART
Athens

Nikolaos and Aikaterini (Dolly) Goulandris founded this museum so they could house their collection of Cycladic and ancient Greek art, including marble figurines, jewellery, vases and other objects from the archaic, classical and Byzantine eras. The Goulandrises worked with archaeologists to catalogue the pieces, and established a foundation for the study of Aegean cultures. Today, the white marble and granite building also showcases contemporary works on a rotational basis: from Henry Moore and Picasso, to Sarah Lucas and Cindy Sherman. The gift shop is a treasure trove of tasteful, Cycladic-inspired design items too.
cycladic.gr

MUSEUM

ALEKOS FASSIANOS
Athens

Set inside a 1960s apartment building in Athens' bohemian Metaxourgeio neighbourhood, this museum dedicated to artist Alekos Fassianos was once the site of his family home, where he resided for decades. The artist, known for his colourful paintings and lithographs inspired by mythology, worked on the interiors with the help of Samos-born architect Kyriakos Krokos. The pair curated and designed everything on display, from the the works on the walls, to minor details including light fixtures and door handles. Since the museum opened in 2023, one year after Fassianos's death, his daughter Viktoria has been running the institution.
alekosfassianos.gr

129

GOULANDRIS MUSEUM OF CONTEMPORARY ART
Athens

The Goulandris family have had an outsized impact on Greece's cultural sector: as well as the Museum of Cycladic Art and the Goulandris Natural History Museum, they are also behind this institution in Pangrati. Opened in 2019, it houses the art collection of the late shipping magnate Basil Goulandris and his wife Elise. Pieces by impressionist, modernist and post-war art heavyweights from Degas to Bacon and Pollock occupy five floors, alongside a café, shop and a library containing over 7,000 books, including those from the couple's personal collection.
goulandris.gr

Legacy issues

To house the collection, a 1920s mansion was renovated and extended with a large, geometric sand-hued annex. A completely new building had originally been planned, but this was abandoned after early excavations at the site revealed it had previously been the home of Aristotle's Lyceum, founded in 335 BCE.

MUSEUM
VORRES MUSEUM
Athens

MUSEUM
MOCA
Andros

Nestled in the remote suburb of Paiania, the Vorres Museum requires some determination to get to. But within the three-acre compound, visitors will find an ethnographic museum with thousands of fascinating, traditional Greek everyday objects and examples of folk art, as well as a modern wing with a top-notch collection of works from the 20th-century avant-garde. The museum's history began in 1964, when Ian Vorres returned to his hometown from studies abroad and found Greek society being rapidly transformed by urbanisation and modernity. He purchased two 19th-century villas and started buying up old furniture and knick-knacks, eventually amassing a collection of around 6,000 items that are exhibited in a domestic setting. Vorres was also an astute collector of contemporary art, which is now displayed in a separate wing built in the 1970s. Despite having been donated to the Greek state, the museum is still headed by Nektarios Vorres, grandson of Ian, and also stages temporary exhibitions.
vorresmuseum.gr

In 1979, Andros native Basil Goulandris and his wife Elise opened the doors to the Museum of Contemporary Art (MOCA) in the island's main town. They intended to establish a small gallery that could host the works of Andros-born sculptor Michael Tombros and show off local talent – with the dream of eventually housing international works. Visitors have since been able to admire the 300 Greek works of its permanent collection, as well as major pieces by Rodin, Kandinsky and Matisse within its white walls. Originally designed by Stamos Papadakis, the building had a new wing added in 1986, where international exhibitions are hosted.
goulandris.gr

MUSEUM
THE OLD OIL MILL
Elefsina, Attica

Elefsina has a weighty history. It was the site of the Eleusinian Mysteries, the annual rites attended by Plato, Plutarch and Roman emperors. More recently, however, the port town became an industrial centre so polluted it gained the unsavoury nickname "the trash can of Athens". A long clean-up is underway and the city is now home to an offbeat arts scene, boosted by Elefsina's turn as a European Capital of Culture in 2023. The city's main venue is the Old Oil Mill, a former soap factory built in 1875. In 1995, the abandoned building was taken over by Aeschylia, Elefsina's homegrown art festival. After a renovation, the building is set to house the town's archaeological museum, currently squeezed into a hilltop villa (its sculpture-strewn courtyard, set against Elefsina's factory chimneys, was immortalised by Henri Cartier-Bresson in 1953). Elefsina's archaeological site – including the temples used in the Eleusinian Mysteries and the mythical well of Demeter – is an essential stop for any antiquity buff.
Kanellopoulou 1, Elefsina

MUSEUM
KOUNDOURIOTIS HISTORICAL MANSION
Hydra

Hydra is home to many illustrious and historical 18th-century stone manors. Built in 1780, the mansion that was the home of of former ship captain Lazaros Koundouriotis is of particular interest as it hosted the revolutionaries of the Greek War of Independence, a cause for which Lazaros provided men, ships and his fortune. A political epicentre for the cause, the building also witnessed the formation of the post-revolution Greek government. Lazaros' great-grandson Pandelis Koundouriotis gifted the house to the state in 1979; today, it hosts a rich collection from the Kountouriotis family's travels within its ochre walls.
Hydra 18040

MUSEUM
HERAKLION ARCHAEOLOGICAL MUSEUM
Heraklion, Crete

Crete was home to a highly advanced prehistoric civilisation, the Minoans, who sent merchants to Egypt and Anatolia and developed at least two distinct written scripts. The Heraklion Archaeological Museum is the main depository of the treasures excavated from the island's many Minoan palaces. Visitors can admire clay statuettes, tableware, fragments of frescoes, jewellery and undeciphered stone tablets covering over five millennia. The museum is housed in a light-filled building in the international style built by Greek architect Patroklos Karantinos between 1937 and 1940.
heraklionmuseum.gr

Under the Ottoman
Crete has a particularly rich archaeological record. During the Ottoman occupation of Greece – which lasted nearly four centuries – the island had the good fortune to be a practically autonomous state within the empire. This meant few precious artefacts were removed and taken abroad.

MUSEUM

YANNOULIS HALEPAS MUSEUM
Tinos

MUSEUM

MUSEUM OF PHOTOGRAPHY
Thessaloniki

This diminutive museum in the town of Pyrgos – the biggest centre for marble production in Tinos, an island known around the country for this industry – is the former home and studio of Yannoulis Halepas, perhaps the most celebrated (and tormented) sculptor in the nation's history. Born in the mid-19th century to a family of stonecutters, Halepas went on to establish himself as what some call "Greece's Rodin", though his worsening mental health led to him spending years in a Corfiot psychiatric hospital and in self-imposed isolation. Other than hosting some of his works, this charming, humble residence has remained virtually unchanged since he lived here in the 1930s and features his personal objects, from clothing to photographs, as well as fascinating sketches and drawings. Besides providing insight into his creative process, his complicated biography and difficult relationship with his parents, it's a great way to get a glimpse of rural life in the Cyclades around a century ago.
Pyrgos 842 01

Thessaloniki's old port has become a bohemian cultural promenade thanks to its many red-brick warehouses that host some of the city's best artistic institutions. Other than the Cinema Museum and screening studios used during the film festival, you'll also find the Museum of Photography here, the only gallery in Greece solely dedicated to the medium. The museum was founded in 1998 and inside there's a collection of 90,000 documents and objects, extensive depositories from Greek photographers such as Aris Georgiou and Socrates Iordanidis, as well as works by international talents such as Swiss-born Frédéric Boisonnas.
momus.gr

POLYCENTRIC MUSEUM OF AIGAI
Vergina

In the north of the country, not far from Thessaloniki, Aigai (today known as Vergina) was formerly the first city of ancient Macedonia. Archaeologists discovered a series of royal tombs here in 1977 and preserved them in situ, rebuilding the space as a museum. The wealth of artefacts and treasures on display provides a fascinating insight into everyday life in the Macedonian kingdom. The fragments of friezes and *heroons* (shrines) are staggering in their delicacy. Marble and ivory statues, gilded military garb, silverware, vases and jewellery sit alongside ceremonial treasures. *aigai.gr*

Buried treasure
Visiting the site requires going underground to where the burial ceremonies occurred. Both King Philip II, father of Alexander the Great, and Alexander IV, the latter's son, were buried here. The site was awarded Unesco World Heritage status in 1996, with restorations of the museum completed in 2022.

DISCOVER GREECE | MUSEUMS

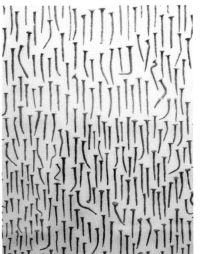

COMMERCIAL GALLERY
THE BREEDER
Athens

Athens is touted as a haven for artists, who are increasingly moving to the city to find affordable studio space – and the commercial gallery scene is growing alongside them. The Breeder, founded in 2002 by George Vamvakidis and Stathis Panagoulis, is an important player on the international scene and has long been a trend-setter. In 2008 it moved to Metaxourgio, the city's gritty red-light district, which today is bustling with arts spaces. There it is housed in a 1970s ice cream factory that was converted into a sleek exhibition space by architect Aris Zampikos.

thebreedersystem.com

Work in progress
On The Breeder's roster are Athens-based artists such as Georgia Sagri and Maria Joannou, but it also deals in works by the likes of British artist and designer Luke Edward Hall and the late Milanese artist Lisa Ponti. The Breeder also runs a residency programme and an open studio, where the space is transformed into an artist's workshop that can be visited by appointment.

COMMERCIAL GALLERY
SYLVIA KOUVALI
Piraeus

ART VENUE
DEO
Chios

To the southwest of Athens, the once-gritty port district of Piraeus has become a hub for commercial art galleries. World-renowned Greek gallerist Sylvia Kouvali was one of the first to set up here in 2018, making the move from Istanbul to the harbour setting. Displayed against exposed brick walls, the pieces in this high-ceilinged space come courtesy of artists hailing from the surrounding eastern Mediterranean, including Egypt, Lebanon and, of course, Greece. There's room for creatives from further afield, too: past exhibitions include shows by Milanese artist Liliana Moro and American avant-garde filmmaker Leslie Thornton.
sylviakouvali.com

"Chios has a rich and complex history, untouched by tourism, allowing it to preserve its authenticity and stories," says Akis Kokkinos (*pictured on left*), who started Deo in 2017 as a personal project inspired by hosting artist friends at his summer home on the island. Now a non-profit organisation, Deo presents a range of free initiatives, including artist residencies, exhibitions and collaborations with local museums and historical sites. "We aim to offer artists something beyond the conventional," adds Kokkinos. What started as a small endeavour with a few hundred attendees has now grown to attract thousands of visitors to the island.
deoprojects.com

DESTE
Hydra

Without Deste, the former slaughterhouse that houses this gallery would have been left to decay. "The artists can't ignore the building's identity. It can be a challenge but also an immense opportunity to see their work in a different way," says founder and Greek-Cypriot art collector Dakis Joannou. Despite choosing Geneva as the location to establish the non-profit Deste Foundation in 1983, Joannou opened its first permanent space in Athens to house his vast collection. A short stroll from Hydra town, this outpost opened in 2009 and every year it hosts an impressive roster of contemporary artists for site-specific shows in its diminutive exhibition space, which clings to the craggy coastline. Among those who have displayed their works here there are big names from George Condo to Pipilotti Rist and Jeff Koons. The latter's Macedonian-style bronze sun sculpture has adorned the roof of the gallery since 2022, glinting as it catches the golden light and spinning with the sea breeze.
deste.gr

LA CHAPELLE SAINT-ANTOINE
Naxos

"When Father George showed us around the Agios Georgios Chapel, we immediately felt a peaceful and nurturing atmosphere conducive to creation," recalls Benjamin Cazeaux-Entremont, co-founder of La Chapelle Saint-Antoine. The idea to establish an artists' residency on Naxos took shape in 2021, when his family began restoring the space to host international artists across disciplines. Since then, La Chapelle has hosted over 40 creatives and expanded its influence, with the annual Villa Apollonia exhibition open to the public. "Through their research projects, residents also form connections with locals," adds Cazeaux-Entremont.
lachapellesaintantoine.com

ART SPACE PYTHAGORION
Samos

Previously a 1970s modernist hotel, the structure now housing Art Space Pythagorion was acquired by the Schwarz Foundation and transformed by local architects Peni Petrakou and Stelios Loulourgas. After extensive renovation, it reopened as an exhibition space in 2012. Alongside artist residencies, the structure is used for everything from installations to film screenings and bazaars. Annual summer exhibitions that have debuted here have gone on to travel to big-name venues from the Kunsthalle Mulhouse in Switzerland to the Athens Conservatoire.
schwarzfoundation.com

Edgy creatives
Art Space Pythagorion sits not only at the edge of the island of Samos but also at the fringes of Europe. From the pier next to the space, visitors can see mainland Turkey. It's a fitting location for a non-profit organisation aiming to encourage the exchange of ideas and practices across borders – as well as reflecting on issues from overfishing to pollution.

DISCOVER GREECE | ART VENUES

MUSIC VENUE

OLD CARPET FACTORY
Hydra

Overlooking the harbour of Hydra, 350 stone steps up from the port, the Old Carpet Factory was originally a workshop for rug weaving. Today it has turned into a music studio and artist residency, founded by Stephan Colloredo-Mansfeld in 2015. Inspired by his bohemian upbringing on the island, the writer, producer and collector of psychedelic vinyl and rare musical instruments transformed part of his 18th-century mansion into a space where musicians could escape modern distractions and embrace experimentation. "We support musicians by offering an environment that inspires creativity on a remote island, miraculously untouched by time," says Colloredo-Mansfeld. "Few restrictions and limitations provide the exact freedom a creative person needs. The Old Carpet Factory has become a place where anarchy and order coexist, allowing artists to feel unconstrained without losing their way." Complimentary live events and exhibitions are also open to the public.
oldcarpetfactory.com

RECORD SHOP

UNDERFLOW
Athens

Vassilis Filippakopoulos opened Underflow in 2015 at the height of the financial crisis, but his brave move paid off. In the two-storey shop, complete with marble floors and concrete walls, you'll find his varied selection of LPs that range from avant-garde jazz to contemporary classical, electronic, indie rock and even Byzantine music. The basement plays host to gigs and exhibitions, which take place every other week. Depending on the time of day, you can dig through the crates while sipping on either an espresso or a cocktail. Underflow also plays an active role in the capital's music scene with its own imprint, which releases records from local artists.
underflow.gr

RECORD SHOP
STEREODISC
Thessaloniki

From Sephardic folk to Balkan beats and Turkish tunes, music has been woven into Thessaloniki's social fabric for centuries, echoing generations of migration. Former radio producer and co-owner Kosmas Efremidis took over Stereodisc in 1984, keen to maintain the soul of the place that piqued his early interest in collecting. Efremidis keeps a close eye on new releases, introducing around 60 new artists onto the shelves each week. His collection is eclectic: you'll find everything from Amy Winehouse and Pink Floyd to Bon Entendeur, the Kyiv Chamber Choir and Afro Disco. *Aristotelous 4, Thessaloniki*

I will survive
In the 1990s, when every Thessaloniki neighbourhood had its own record store, Greece's second city became an incubator of emerging talent, particularly for rock, jazz and neoclassical artists. Today, Stereodisc is one of only two remaining music shops in town. Established in 1968, it is also one of the oldest in Europe.

IN FOCUS
OPEN-AIR CINEMAS
Thrills for everyone

Outdoor entertainment is synonymous with the Greek lifestyle and nothing beats watching a movie on the big screen under a starry sky. Greece's alfresco cinemas, or *therina*, have become an institution since their first appearance in the early 1900s and have shaped the nation's collective consciousness on the meaning of a summer evening. All generations flock to these secret gardens dotted with canvas chairs to take in films projected on a screen, framed by fragrant honeysuckle and jasmine vines. The noisy crunch of footsteps rushing over the gravel to grab a seat is the unofficial signal that the movie is about to start.

The motion picture first came to Greece at the end of the 19th century. Summer cinemas followed a few years later when enterprising *provolatzides* (screeners) started unrolling large white cloths on which they would project a movie for Athenians sitting at cafés in the capital's main square. At its peak in the 1960s, 500 such cinemas were in operation; today some 100 remain in the Athens region alone. Outdoor cinemas are found in both private and public spaces, including terraces and gardens. Open-air film festivals have showcased movies in the unlikeliest of places – from basketball courts and schoolyards to beaches and ancient ruins.

1

Picture perfect
Across the country, nearly every part of Greece boasts its own charming summer cinema. There is a *therino* for everyone, whether you love blockbusters or art-house movies but here are some of the most engaging.

1 Santorini Cinema
2 Mykonos Cinemanto
3 Cine Kipos, Chania
4 Cine Thisio, Athens
5 Cine Paris, Athens

1 Tickets please!
2 Kipos Municipal Cinema, Chania
3 Edge of the seat stuff
4 Silver screen: Cine Manto, Mykonos
5 Epic scenes: Cine Paris, Athens
6 Service with a smile

3

4

5   6

BOOKSHOP

ADAD BOOKS
Athens

In leafy Merkouri Square, Adad is a bookshop and café founded by Belgian Alix Janta-Polczynski (*pictured*). Since 2022, it has become a go-to spot for readers and coffee lovers. "It was empty since I moved to Athens and I used to walk by and think it would make the cutest bookshop," she says. As luck would have it, it was owned by her neighbour's sister, who agreed to its transformation into a cosy spot to browse titles and sip coffee from Athenian roastery Area 51. Janta-Polczynski also runs art space Alkinois and the café displays works by artists she has shown – including illustrations painted directly onto the walls by French artist Cham Lavant.
Anteou 1, Athens

BOOKSHOP

HYPER HYPO
Athens

When Andreas Kokkino and Stathis Mitropoulos (*pictured*) opened Hyper Hypo in Athens' Monastiraki neighbourhood in 2021, all they were trying to do was create the kind of space that they wanted in the area. "Somebody had to do it," says Kokkino. Since then, the bookshop has been a hit with residents and tourists alike. From the latest graphic novels to cutting-edge photography titles, classic and contemporary theoretical texts and art tomes, the razor-sharp selection strikes a balance between playful and profound. On the shelves you'll also find a selection of publications about the nation itself that are very popular with customers. "If the word 'Greece' is in the title, it will sell," adds Kokkino. Among the most eagerly sought-after books are the pocket-sized editions by small imprint Kyklàda, that explore subjects from the aesthetics of Greek sculpture to the architecture of Cycladic holiday homes. It's a space that feels as much a bookshop as it does a talking shop for the city's flourishing art and design scene.
hyperhypo.gr

BOOKSHOP
ANTILALOS
Tinos

The books in Antilalos are not arranged in any specific order but that's part of the charm of this place. Owners (and sisters) Christina and Sofia Koraki hand-pick unique second-hand and antique titles so the selection never stays the same and rewards the curious. Christina and her husband fell in love with the island in 2016 and relocated from Athens; Sofia and her family followed a year later, when the duo started this venture. Back in the capital, their sister Lena helps hunt for rarities in the city's markets. In the idiosyncratic mix you'll find poetry, classics and philosophy, as well as some novels and children's literature. There's also a handful of new editions dedicated to the island. "We collect what we believe is the best," says Christina. Other than running the in-house café, Sofia is an artist: you can find her hand-painted postcards for sale as well as larger works on display as part of exhibitions on the second floor. A spiral staircase leads to a workshop space in the attic, that hosts classes, yoga, seminars and the occasional movie night.
Paxamadi, Tinos

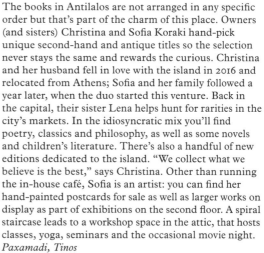

While Greece may have created theatre, philosophy and democracy, it has in no way rested on its laurels since. We talk to three professionals about the country's vibrant modern cultural scene.

MEET THE EXPERTS

SIA KOSIONI
SKAI television news

Sia Kosioni is a journalist and the main anchor with SKAI, one of Greece's biggest private news channels.

What is your favourite aspect of Greek culture?
Greek culture develops around a dining table with good food and wine. This is where families and friends meet, talk, laugh and cry. It's also where they come together, express love, confess problems, admit mistakes, make small and big deals and of course fight about politics.

What makes Greece's media industry unique?
We have more media than we can consume, while at the same time it's never enough. Of course, the internet is booming, but traditional media is still relevant and influential. Greek TV is a bubbly place, flooded with news shows hosting debates that never come to a conclusion and bulletins longer than those in India with its population of 1.4 billion. I anchor one of them.

What are the issues that Greek people care about most?
Definitely politics. People love to hate politics in Greece. If you ask, they will say that they need more coverage of everyday issues. But if you ask me as a professional, it is with politics that the Greek soul sparkles. Always a good reason for hard debates with friends or family – don't forget, this is where democracy was born.

KATERINA VRANA
Comedian

Katerina Vrana is a comedian who was left with serious injuries following an accident in Malaysia – and then made a hit show out of it. She performs all over the world, in both Greek and English.

What makes Greece's comedy scene special?
The Greek comedy scene is a little diamond in the rough. I find it amazing that within such a small number of comedians – about 40 – you can find a very high standard in nearly every type of comedy. We were among the first non-English-speaking stand-up comedians to perform abroad in their native language. This is extra impressive when you consider the small population Greece has: around 10 million. We spread surprisingly far and wide for such a small number of people.

Who are the most exciting names in the Greek comedy scene?
Apart from me, you mean? It's difficult to narrow it down because so many Greek comedians are doing something exciting at the moment. Whether developing their material in new ways, branching out to performing in English, playing bigger venues, writing and producing TV series... I truly believe that amazing things will come out of Greece very soon. Watch this space.

Why should people visit Greece?
Well, apart from wonderful beaches, the beautiful sea, vibrant city centres, the amazing Greek inland and mountains (which are still fairly unexplored by tourists), I would say visit Greece to meet the Greeks. Apparently, Greece has a plummeting birth rate and pessimistic predictions say that there won't be many Greeks left soon. So hurry up and catch us while you can.

ODETTE KOUZOU
Thermia Project

Odette Kouzou is a curator and the founder of Thermia Project, an artist residency on the island of Kythnos. The project was founded in 2022 and aims to marry contemporary art with traditional crafts and methods.

What makes Greece's arts scene unique?
In the last few years, it has become much more diverse and vibrant. There is a growing demand for emerging talent, and Greece has a strong foundation, heavily influenced by the country's rich history. Foreign artists moving here and engaging with this dynamic movement have also contributed to a lively and fresh scene with great potential for the future.

Who are the most exciting artists working in Greece today?
I have a deep appreciation for many artists, who inspired me to found Thermia Project. My main focus is on collaborating with, and supporting, emerging artists by providing them with the time and space to work. Some of the creatives I admire and have followed over the years include Antonakis Christodoulou, Ioanna Limniou, Konstantinos Mouchtaridis, Despina Charitonidi and Alexandros Simopoulos, among others.

Why should people visit Greece?
For its breathtaking landscapes along with its rich cultural experiences. It's one of those places where nature, ancient ruins and folklore meet contemporary life and art, with each region offering something unique.

Greece's history is witnessed across its landscape and today's architects use this legacy as inspiration: here is our round up of remarkable structures, both ancient and modern.

ARCHITECTURE

Greece's most impressive architectural projects are the consequence of a dialogue between old and new, where modern structures pay homage to their classical predecessors. Everywhere, the most striking buildings are those that know how to intersect with the landscape. A case in point is the New Acropolis Museum: an elegant, quasi-brutalist design by Bernard Tschumi that frames views of the Parthenon with a glass-walled gallery, linking ancient and contemporary in one stroke. Yet Greece's commitment to innovation doesn't overshadow its reverence for the past. The ancient Theatre of Epidaurus, whose design gives flawless acoustics, still hosts performances without the need for microphones. Modernist architect Dimitris Pikionis's intervention into the Loumbardiaris Chapel also shows a profound respect for history. Modern Greece is both forward-thinking and rooted in its heritage. These spaces echo bygone eras while pushing the boundaries of design. Let's take a tour.

THE EDIT

1 **Villa Mâche**
Modernist villa designed in exile.

2 **Stavros Niarchos Foundation Cultural Centre**
A vast, clean-slate public project.

3 **Loumbardiaris Chapel**
Thoughtful restoration of a 17th century church using modern methods.

4 **New Acropolis Museum**
Successful modern counterpoint to a world-famous ancient structure.

5 **Chios Mastic Museum**
Unobtrusive addition to a rare landscape.

6 **Theatre of Epidaurus**
A masterpiece of classical acoustics.

7 **Lakki Cinema**
Artifact from an overlooked era of Dodecanese history.

8 **Euphoria Retreat**
Striking spa complex built into a hill.

9 **Environment Museum of Stymphalia**
Part of the environment it highlights.

10 **Thessaloniki waterfront**
Greece's second city gets a new look.

11 **Agora Modiano**
Thessaloniki's reborn market building.

RESIDENTIAL BUILDING
VILLA MÂCHE
Amorgos

Villa Mâche's architect, Iannis Xenakis, built the house for his daughter and her husband, the French composer François-Bernard Mâche. He was influenced as much by the whitewashed houses of the Cyclades, of which Amorgos is the easternmost island, as by the work of modernist master Le Corbusier, with whom Xenakis had worked. The residence is made up of five separate structures, each carved with slim windows to let the light in. Xenakis designed the house in 1967, having to rely on photos of the site after he was exiled from Greece in 1947 for deserting the army. It took a further seven years for the house to be built and it was finally completed in 1974.

CULTURAL CENTRE
STAVROS NIARCHOS FOUNDATION CULTURAL CENTRE
Athens

Glass-fronted and angular, the Stavros Niarchos Foundation Cultural Centre in Kallithea is a landmark structure in both culture and philanthropy. In 2008, the Greek state handed Italian architect Renzo Piano a plot of land, asking him to compose a cutting-edge, multifunctional arts, entertainment and educational space.

Today, the SNFCC hosts the National Library of Greece, as well as an opera wing that contains two auditoria, with a total of 1,850 seats between them. The roof, which is supported by thin metal columns, holds a carpet of solar panels, helping the entire building to run on sustainable energy come rain or shine.

LOUMBARDIARIS CHAPEL
Athens

Overseen by the Acropolis, the site of Church of Saint Demetrios Loumbardiaris is believed to have hosted churches since the 9th century, though the structure there today is from the mid-1600s. It is not Athens' oldest church, but it is certainly one of the most charming – thanks to a 1955 restoration by renowned modernist architect Demetrios Pikionis. Pikionis added a gate and pavillion around the church that merge the aesthetics of Japan and ancient Byzantium into a minimalist hybrid; he also reworked the rear exterior wall with intricate stonework. Inside, a series of intricate frescoes and adornments inspire a sense of reverence and tranquillity.

NEW ACROPOLIS MUSEUM
Athens

Set at the foot of the Acropolis, this museum was designed by Paris-based Bernard Tschumi Architects and opened after eight years of development and construction. Unusually, the ground floor of the gallery is sloped, replicating the orientation of the Parthenon itself, while excavated sites are seen through glass floor panels. The sculpture gallery, where marble torsos are shown between concrete columns, is where the combination of contemporary and ancient is at its most effective. In the Parthenon gallery the ingenious display mounts a frieze from the monument on a central cube, with a second layer of exhibits wrapped around it.

MUSEUM
CHIOS MASTIC MUSEUM
Chios

This subtle building is half-buried in the landscape so as not to disturb the ancient environment responsible for its existence. With its cantilevered, slatted-wood roof and tree trunk-like, Y-shaped supporting columns, the museum was designed by Greek architects Kizi Studio and sits at the heart of a vast grove of mastic trees, the plant from which mastic gum – a valuable traditional remedy and flavouring popular across the eastern Mediterranean – is produced. Chios is the only site in the region where *skínos* (as the tree is known in Greece) is still cultivated, part of a labour-intensive agricultural tradition dating back to the 14th century.

THEATRE
THEATRE OF EPIDAURUS
Epidaurus, Peloponnese

The Theatre of Epidaurus is the definition of standing the test of time. Built in the late 4th century BCE, it is still used and has a capacity of 14,000. In the summer, the theatre taps into its heritage for the Athens and Epidaurus Festival, hosting Greek dramas such as tragedies by Euripides and Sophocles, and comedies by Aristophanes. Polykleitos the Younger, the architect who conceived of the structure, intended that a pin dropped on stage should be heard even in the uppermost seats. Remarkable as this is, perhaps the most impressive aspect of Polykleitos' work is how well it is integrated into the hillside, overlooking the sanctuary of Asklepios.

CINEMA

LAKKI CINEMA
Leros

Leros is home to architectural reminders of a forgotten chapter in Greek history. The Dodecanese group was ceded to Italy in 1912 and in 1923 they started building a naval base on Leros that required a new town for its personnel. To achieve this, two modernist architects, Rodolfo Petracco and Armando Bernabiti, were sent to construct a "utopia" at Lakki. Rationalism – the style they used, with purposeful, plain aesthetics intended to express Italian fascist values – has since been rehabilitated, despite its thorny political associations. The most notable remaining example is Lakki's cinema, with its pale colouring and clean, straight lines.

155

LEISURE COMPLEX
EUPHORIA RETREAT
Mystras, Peloponnese

Euphoria Retreat is hidden in the heart of the Peloponnese, not far from the 13th-century town of Mystras and its Byzantine churches. The latter provided inspiration for the resort's centrepiece, designed by Deca Architecture: an extraordinary spherical pool painted in shades of blue and green that reflect the colours of Byzantine dome murals. All of the spa's wet areas sit at the lowest level in this four-storey building that steps down the steep hill, with each floor buried progressively deeper into the earth. Above ground, inside a revamped 1830s mansion, 45 rooms have also been designed to a palette that references Byzantine frescoes.

ENVIRONMENT MUSEUM OF STYMPHALIA
Stymphalia, Corinthia

The Environment Museum of Stymphalia is perhaps the best "thematic" museum in Greece. In mythology, this was the location of Hercules' sixth trial, where he shot down the man-eating birds of Stymphalia with a bow and arrow. The museum would condone no such behaviour today. Celebrating the natural world, it raises ecological awareness and highlights the folkloric history of the region. Informative as this is, the most impressive feature of the museum is its exterior platform, which wraps around the building. It's only right for a museum that champions the environment to have such a spectacular view onto the lush surrounding mountains.

THESSALONIKI WATERFRONT
Thessaloniki

A landmark revitalisation project for Greece and beyond, Thessaloniki's waterfront is a 3.5km-long landscaped space featuring 13 distinct "garden rooms". Each offers something different in the way of sun, shade, structures and a wide variety of native Mediterranean plants. If you begin at the iconic White Tower, walking south you'll come across the Royal Theatre: thereafter, you'll happen on skate parks, basketball and tennis courts, and gardens themed around music, water, memory and sound. Of the monuments and artworks, the most impressive is 'The Umbrellas', a flock of 13m-high accessories, rendered in metal by Greek sculptor George Zongolopoulos.

MARKET
AGORA MODIANO
Thessaloniki

The Great Fire of Thessaloniki in 1917 destroyed two-thirds of the city, including its main market: the Agora Modiano. Originally built on the site of a former synagogue for the city's once-large Jewish community, the market building was reconstructed and completed in 1930. It has since been the centre of Thessaloniki's public life and reputation as a gastronomic destination. With its neat columns, arches and pediments, the facade echoes the architecture of Greek antiquity. A recent renovation maintained the building's character, with street food carts and delis now sitting next to traditional produce stalls that have supplied residents for almost a century.

Within its borders Greece contains a truly remarkable geographical diversity. From stark, volcanic coastlines to lush, sheer-sided river valleys, here is a list of some of its treasures.

THE GREAT OUTDOORS

Thanks to its obliging climate, Greece offers a masterclass in outdoor living. The mainland is flush with rugged peaks, most notably the Pindus range. Hikers will meet wild goats on trails that wind through ancient forests and past crystalline lakes. For a more leisurely pace, the Peloponnese has vineyards and olive groves, perfect for a country amble followed by a wine tasting. But the islands are where Greece comes into its own. Each is unique: from the pine-scented coves of the Ionian islands to the rugged beaches of the Aegean, all are ideal for sailing, with many spots accessible only by boat. You can kayak or paddleboard next to seals in Alonissos or turtles in Kefalonia – or dive to explore ruins and shipwrecks. For those seeking solitude, Greece's lesser-known regions, such as Epirus and Evia, offer untouched natural landscapes. Come winter, those mountains have great skiing too. Whatever the season, there are opportunities for both adventure and tranquillity.

THE EDIT

1 Beaches
One of the features that made Greek holidays famous, here are some stunning places where the land, sea and sky meet.

2 Beach clubs
Spots to relax or party in, depending on the hour.

3 Natural regions
A list of areas of outstanding natural beauty.

4 Skiing
Our pick of the best of Greece's impressive mountain resorts.

BEACH
AVLAKI
Hydra

The best time for a dip at Avlaki is around 08.30, when you're likely to have the whole place to yourself, though it is equally beautiful to linger at sunset. A few minutes walk from Hydra town, this spot (it is not a sandy beach, in common with most of the rest of the island) is reached via a hill path and a staircase, which are worth the descent. When you reach your destination, the concrete ledge set up for swimmers has a convenient ladder into the water, which spares you from navigating the rocks. The sea is refreshing and crystalline, making this place appealing for either a quick plunge or a languid afternoon spent around the cove.

BEACH
SARAKINIKO
Milos

The unique topography of Sarakiniko comes from the almost-white volcanic rock that has been sculpted into mounds and craters by millennia of erosion from the wind and waves. Exploring the surface and caves of this lunar-like terrain is encouraged (as long as footwear permits) as there are rock pools, snorkelling coves and opportunities to cliff jump. Equidistant from Milos's capital, Plaka and the nearby town of Adamas, it is a popular spot but rarely feels crowded due to its spectacular vastness. There is minimal shade on Sarakiniko but the dazzling contrast between the stone and the sea ensures you will have a memorable visit.

BEACH
RED BEACHES
Santorini

Each year, Santorini fills up with visitors seeking panoramic views from its five-star hotels. However, the island also has a rugged, rustic side and its red rock beaches are proof. Other than the titular Red Beach in the island's south, you will also find this volcanic, burnt-brick coloured sand at Armeni, close to the town of Oia.

BEACH
CHERONISSOS
Sifnos

Nestled at the northern tip of the island of Sifnos, Cheronissos is a remote harbour a short drive from Apollonia – though, of course, arriving by boat is the most scenic way to reach the bay. Cheronissos has surprisingly few visitors and the hills on either side protect it from the wind. Sitting on the beach, you can watch the fishing boats gently rock on the water, whilst the two tavernas on the shore serve the fishermen's catches for lunch. Both have tables right by the sea or you can choose to eat in the shade of a native tamarisk tree. There's an old-school ceramics workshop on the sand, too, if you're after a charming, hand-made souvenir.

AGIOS NIKOLAOS
Symi

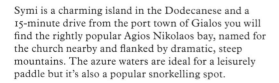

Symi is a charming island in the Dodecanese and a 15-minute drive from the port town of Gialos you will find the rightly popular Agios Nikolaos bay, named for the church nearby and flanked by dramatic, steep mountains. The azure waters are ideal for a leisurely paddle but it's also a popular snorkelling spot.

ATHENS RIVIERA BEACH CLUBS
Athens

On the pine-clad Vouliagmeni peninsula, this stretch of Athenian real estate is now home to a five-star resort, an exclusive marina, a Nobu restaurant and two of the most desirable beach clubs on the Athenian riviera. On the west side of the peninsula, Astir Beach Club has been attracting glamorous residents since the late 1950s. The nearby Four Seasons Astir Hotel *(see page 40)* boasts some of Greece's most luxurious amenities. Guests can enjoy water sports or visit Astir Marina to spot jet-setters and Athens' elite. A short walk away, The Royal Beach Vouliagmeni Club blends modern design with Mediterranean elegance, offering loungers, fine dining and impeccable service for a perfect day by the sea.

BEACH CLUB
ALEMAGOU
Mykonos

Beach bar and restaurant Alemagou has been designed so the furnishings complement its surroundings. The restaurant serves a fusion version of Aegean classics, including showstoppers like lobster spaghetti. Save some energy for sunset, when Alemagou draws famous DJs, turning it from beach club, to club on the beach.

BEACH CLUB
CIEL
Syros

With its neoclassical palaces and pastel façades, Syros has a unique feel among the Cyclades. Just steps away from Ermoupolis's centre, Ciel is a seafront bar and restaurant built into the rock face, with comfortable cabanas on decking by the water. From dawn to dusk the view is unparalleled but it is best enjoyed at golden hour.

LAKE VOULIAGMENI
Athens

ARCADIA
Peloponnese

In the mountainous Peloponnese, Arcadia is an area of quaint villages and unspoiled landscapes. Perched on the sprawling 75km Menalon Trail, the ancient Monastery of Prodromos (*below*) is precariously built into the rock face; further down the route, hikers will also find the fascinating (and labyrinthine) Kapsia caves.

Sitting just inland from the coast on the Athenian Riviera, Lake Vouliagmeni is always pleasantly warm. Thanks to the geothermal springs in the underwater cave network that stretches over 4.2km around its basin, the lake's brackish water (a combination of fresh and sea water) remains between 21 and 29C all year round. The lounging and swimming facilities at the main deck are open every day for those wanting an impromptu dip but there are also private areas, as well as a restaurant and a wealth of restorative spa treatments. Encircled by dramatic limestone cliffs, the emerald lake's mineral-rich waters are believed to have healing benefits and beckon those looking for a break from the area's sandy beaches.

NATURAL REGION
ZAGOROCHORIA
Zagori

Spread across 46 remote villages known collectively as Zagorochoria, this is one of the largest municipalities in northwestern Greece and one of the least densely populated areas in the whole country. Owing to its status as a Unesco World Heritage Site, skiing is not permitted in the winter but rafting, horse riding and mountain biking are encouraged as alternate ways to enjoy the rugged scenery. Trekking up the Vikos gorge will lead you to the Voidomatis river, one of the clearest and deepest in Europe, where you can count the iconic stone bridges along the route. If you make it up to the Oxya viewpoint and Dragon lake, stop off for the night at Katikia guest house.

SKIING
MOUNTAIN RESORTS
Gems in high places

You're only as cold as you feel
The Freeride World Tour choses to
host their 2024 off-piste qualifying
competition on the Helmos mountain,
attracting the best snowboarders
from around the world. Parnassos has
the most lively après scene and the
thrum of DJ sets echoes through the
mountains in the afternoon there.

Most visitors come to Greece for summer sun, so they might
not realise it is also well-equipped for snow. The mountains
of the Peloponnese peninsula boast excellent skiing resorts
and are guaranteed to be less busy than their Alpine
competitors. One popular destination is Kalavryta Ski Resort
and Helmos Mountain, which can accommodate all levels of
skiers, with 12 runs and seven lifts to choose from. You can
ski here with a view of the sea and those reaching the resort's
lodge at 2,440 metres can see all the way to the Gulf of
Corinth. Further north in the country, Falakro Ski Centre is
a newer resort near the border of Macedonia with 21 slopes
across 22km and a mixture of green, red and black runs.
There are three chalets, one offering accommodation for 86
at the base and one at the top of the four-person chairlift with
panoramic views across Chionotrypa at an altitude of
2,110 metres. Thessaloniki is the nearest airport, but those
choosing the scenic route and arriving by train should aim for
Drama, 45km away. A third option is the Parnassos Ski
Centre at Arachova, near Delphi, the largest resort in Greece.
Here there are two main skiing areas – Kellaria and Fterolakas
– with 21 pistes and five connecting trails. The resort is a
three-hour drive from Athens and those looking for off-piste
and more advanced descents will be well rewarded here.

PART 02

PUT DOWN ROOTS

So, you are considering staying longer – perhaps even settling permanently? Allow us to introduce you to the best areas to consider and professionals to enlist, plus a few people who already made the move.

With an amenable climate, beautiful landscapes, hospitable population and bouyant economy, Greece offers plentiful opportunities for business and a great quality of life. Here are our ideas on where to put down roots.

WHERE TO LIVE

THE VILLAGE IN THE CITY
KOUKAKI
Athens

In the leafy foothills of the Acropolis, Koukaki offers historic character, intriguing architecture and a gentle, relaxed vibe in the heart of Athens.

Population: 645,000 (municipal Athens)
Closest airport: Athens International Airport is about one hour on the metro
Eat: Tuk Tuk
Drink: Kinono
Shop: Ere

Right beneath the Parthenon and pine-covered Hill of the Muses, Koukaki's century-old townhouses, Bauhaus flats and 1960s apartment blocks are steeped in history. Bernard Tschumi's sharply modern Acropolis Museum makes a bold contrast to the antiquities, while EMST, the city's main contemporary art museum, embodies its new cultural identity. Although visitors have increasingly discovered it in the last few years, Koukaki remains staunchly lived-in. Joggers and dog walkers start the day on forested Philoppapou hill, a rare expanse of greenery in the city centre. At street level, breezy cafés (Salute Bistro), meze bars (Svoura), and concept stores (Ere) vye for a young, creative crowd, but traditional *kafenia* and *souvlaki* joints still cater to old timers. Clustered around Veikou, Falirou and Odissea Androutsou streets, a new generation of makers have set up workshops (like Trabala Studio and LoFi Concept), alongside vintage shops and homegrown fashion studios. Well connected but within walking distance of everything, Koukaki is the epitome of old-new Athens.

THE SEASIDE HAVEN
CHANIA
Crete

Wedged between the Sea of Crete and the towering White mountains,
this vibrant university city combines laidback island life and
unpretentious urban buzz.

Population: 54,000
Closest airport: Chania international
airport is a 20-minute drive
Eat: Kafenío Fix
Drink: Vermuteria
Shop: Carmela Iatropoulou

When British painter John Craxton settled in a dilapidated harbourfront studio in Chania in the early 1960s, he brought a bohemian set of artists and outsiders in his wake. Although it is no longer an undiscovered paradise, a new generation of expats are now moving into the heritage buildings and surrounding villages of this lively port city with its intact Venetian old town and modern suburbs. "Hospitality to strangers is the hallmark of Crete," says Nikos Tsepetis, owner of design-led Ammos Hotel (*see page 18*) and Red Jane bakery (*see page 68*). Chania's new archaeological museum has revived the fortunes of Halepa, a headland of parks and mansions, while Tabakaria, the old waterfront tannery area, is home to enterprising restaurants and hotels. Then there's the proximity to ravishing beaches, mountain hamlets with amazing tavernas and incredible hiking and biking terrain. With two international airports and a new highway connecting Chania to the Cretan capital in the pipeline, this sunny coastal city is looking up.

176

THE ISLAND ESCAPE
ERMOUPOLIS
Syros

The stately capital of the Cyclades defies Greek island stereotypes with its
neo-classical palazzos, marble squares and year-round cultural life, luring
an increasingly cosmopolitan population.

Population: 22,000
Closest airport: Syros airport is a
10-minute drive
Eat: Revans
Drink: Theosis
Shop: Prekas

Named after Hermes, the god of merchants, thieves and
travellers, Ermoupolis has been an affluent commercial
and cultural centre ever since Greek refugees from the
Ottoman occupation built shipyards and factories here
in the 19th century. The city's impressive mansions,
theatres and civic infrastructure are their legacy.
Tourism has only recently arrived in this self-sufficient
spot, once jokingly known as the Switzerland of the
Aegean. Despite its urbane atmosphere, the seaside city
is rich in folk culture too. Wooden boats are still built in
the dockyard and musicians play live in the cosy *ouzeri*.
Markos Vamvakaris, the godfather of *rebetika* (the Greek
blues) was born in Ano Syros, a cascade of whitewashed
cottages that crowns the city. With a thriving university,
good schools and co-working spaces for newcomers,
Ermoupolis is attracting a sophisticated set who
value the arts as much as quality of life. Less than an
hour's high-speed ferry ride from Mykonos and its
international airport, this island is alive well after high
season wraps up.

WHERE TO LIVE

PUT DOWN ROOTS

RESIDENCE
PETRALONA HOUSE
Athens

Whatever your architectural tastes and requirements, Greece has something to offer. We look at three examples of inspiring homes, starting with this remarkable family dwelling that draws from a very broad palette.

Architect couple Konstantinos Pantazis and Marianna Rentzou (*pictured*) of Point Supreme (*see page 186*) interwove different colours and forms for their renovation of Petralona House. The couple's update of this 20th-century home drew from surrealist ideals, with a dose of Greek aesthetics. "People often ask, 'Why so many colours?' It's risky but colour is a brilliant way to evoke feeling," says Rentzou. They've kept the façade's French shutters, balcony railings and old-fashioned awnings, but have added dark-blue tiles on the exterior, chequered floor tiles, green bathroom walls, mustard window frames, blood-orange gates and a pink staircase. It may sound like a visual feast but bathing in the Mediterranean sun, the interiors feel remarkably calm. "Contemporary architecture in Greece tends to be modernist, without much 'Greekness'; we wanted to bring back a Greek sensibility," says Pantazis. It's an example of a perfectly mixed aesthetic cocktail for those who value simple, everyday moments with family, and look to do so in an open, visually enticing home.

POLYKATOIKIA
Athens

Adaptable and socially inclusive, Greece's 20th-century multi-residence tower blocks are undergoing a renaissance as their modular nature – a feature of the nation's unique planning laws – receives greater acclaim.

Born in Australia to Greek parents, Nectar Efkarpidis spent his childhood shuttling between continents. He would spend term time in Canberra and enjoyed breaks in Greece, staying with relatives in Thessaloniki. There, the future developer was introduced to *polykatoikia*. Literally translated as "many residences", these modular apartment blocks began to spring up in Greek cities in the 1950s to cater for an influx of residents from the countryside. In 2015, Efkarpidis bought several derelict buildings and apartments, intending to restore and update them for modern living. "I think they're fascinating both architecturally and socially," says Efkarpidis. "Everyone inside knows each other. There are examples where a family would build a house and when their children grew up, the parents would add an upper floor for them. They in turn would build another floor for their own children." The resulting buildings are physical representations of the multi-generational living that has helped regenerate Greek cities by keeping them bonded with family ties.

RESIDENCE

ANDRIA MITSAKOS
Paros

While modern Greek interior design frequently tends towards
modernism and minimalism, cultural collector Andria Mitsakos
shows that there is also an appeal to "maximalism".

On the island of Paros, a small, pastoral retreat stands
in the fields among goats and sheep, filled with objects
from a lifetime of collecting. "I've been called a
maximalist," says Andria Mitsakos, owner of eccentric
Greek design brand, Anthologist (*see page 104*). She
spent the pandemic completing the renovation of this
rustic farmhouse: with an interior designer mother
and an antique dealer aunt, her education in collecting
beautiful objects started early. Inside the stucco-walled
cottage, Mitsakos's desk is supported by two old stone

griffins, topped with a piece of marble that she salvaged
and polished. Nearby, there's a whimsical grasshopper-
shaped Mexican coffee table made of rattan. In her
bedroom, two antique, embroidered silk suzanis from
Central Asia hang on the wall. Her home is a love
letter to Greece; from textiles sourced in Metsovo
and Ioannina in the north, to the wood furniture of
Skyros and Crete and the ceramics found in Athenian
workshops. "There's so much old-world craft still being
made here. It's incredible," she says.

Whether you need a family dwelling, a chic beachfront hotel or a city-centre shop, these are the architects you'll need to make your chosen space sing.

ARCHITECTURE & DESIGN

ARCHITECTURE STUDIO
POINT SUPREME ARCHITECTS
Athens

Point Supreme Architects was founded in Rotterdam in 2008 by Marianna Rentzou and Konstantinos Pantazis, who had spent time in London, Brussels, Tokyo and the Netherlands, working for the likes of OMA and MVRDV. Adept at applying colour and selecting materials with confidence, Point Supreme has turned everything from an unfinished basement to a rooftop dwelling into attractive homes that make clever use of small spaces. "The international experience of living in different cultures and cities with strong identities gave us a fresh, externalised view of Athens, so we are highly sensitive to its uniqueness and potential," says Pantazis.
pointsupreme.com

ARCHITECTURE STUDIO
K-STUDIO
Athens

Of the new wave of Greek architectural talent,
K-Studio is a forerunner. Brothers Dimitris and
Konstantinos Karampatakis studied at The Bartlett
School of Architecture in London and did a stint
with Will Alsop's practice there, before returning to
Athens and starting their studio in 2004. Ever since,
they have fine-tuned their skills by competing for
ambitious commissions, with a portfolio that spans from
commercial to residential. Examples of their work are
peppered through this book, from mountainous hotel
Manna (*see page 32*) to the handsome headquarters of
Metaxa Liknon in Samos (*see page 80*).
k-studio.gr

ARCHITECTURE STUDIO
ETSI ARCHITECTS
Kardamyli

Etsi Architects is a multi-faceted studio established by
award-winning architect Eleni Tsigarida. It is equally
adept at building from scratch as at historic restorations,
melding the Peloponnese's architectural heritage with
modern needs. The practice values sourcing materials
and labour locally, ensuring designs are harmonised
with their surroundings. Olive wood, marble, slate and
local pebbles are all used to ground the properties amid
the Mani peninsula landscape. "We strive to create
spaces that blend traditional charm with contemporary
functionality, all while being deeply client-centric and
environmentally conscious," says Tsigarida.
etsi.design

INTERIOR DESIGN
LAB PIREE SUPERSTUDIO
Piraeus

Lab Piree Superstudio, spearheaded by acclaimed designer Kosmas Karavas, operates out of a converted industrial warehouse that was once an old harbour marine shop in Piraeus. Through a loose, free-form approach, Lab Piree has developed a portfolio of interiors appropriate for all manner of public and private spaces. While the team's speciality is tiling, they also design an eclectic mix of furniture, lighting and homeware. Whether you're looking for an artful refit of a bathroom or to kit out a brand-new kitchen, Lab Piree will provide the option that always strikes the right balance between function and characterful aesthetics.
labpireesuperstudio.com

INTERIOR DESIGN
157+173 DESIGNERS
Thessaloniki

Established in 2009 by architects Babis Papanikolaou and Christina Tsiragelou (who left in 2020) this firm should be sought out by those who are after a quirky, playful approach to interior design. In all their projects and across their extensive directory of products to furnish a new Greek residence – including concrete ceiling lamps and geometric copper light fixtures – the team use simple, eco-friendly materials, resulting in a raw, edgy aesthetic. The studio is also prepared to provide its input on shops, hotels and museums; recent work includes the conversion of an early 20th century tradesman's fabric shop into a unique two-storey home.
157-173designers.eu

MARBLE
ON ENTROPY
Chalandri

Niki and Zoe Moskofoglou (*pictured*), an architect and a civil engineer respectively, studied in the UK and in 2012 it was there they decided to honour the multifaceted character of marble in a collection of furnishings and lighting. The returned to Greece in 2014 and now work in a studio in Chalandri, just north of Athens and not far from the quarry at the foot of Mount Pentelicus where marble was sourced in Greek antiquity. "This marble was used to build the Parthenon – it's particularly white," explains Zoe. As a patron, you will be in good company: the designers' "Cutting Corners" tables already adorn Maximos Mansion, the Greek prime minister's office.
onentropy.com

CARPETS
SOUTZOGLOU CARPETS
Athens

All new arrivals in Athens should swing by Soutzoglou Carpets's showroom, just off Kolonaki Square. Founded as a carpet-weaving workshop by Nicholas Soutzoglou in 1900, today the business is run by his son Kyriacos Soutzoglou and granddaughter Electra Soutzoglou (*pictured*). They offer a collection of antique carpets alongside modern, handmade rugs, including bespoke designs and one-off artists' editions. Clients often come in looking for a neutral-hued modern carpet, but quickly change their mind when presented with an azilal from Morocco or a kilim woven by Tuaregs. "When you come to our showroom, your appetite opens up," says Electra. *soutzoglou.com*

Whether you need to kit out a family dwelling, a chic beachfront hotel or
a city-centre shop, these are the architects you'll need to make
your chosen space sing:

FURNITURE

SET
Athens

Family-owned Set specialises in interior design and
furniture for the hospitality industry. The shop stocks a
well-thought-out collection of products from European
brands, while many of its own pieces are made using
reclaimed teak from Indonesia. Its latest venture is a
line of outdoor furniture produced in Greece, using one
of the country's most abundant resources: aluminium.
Featuring striped cushions, with recycled fabric sourced
from Colours of Arley in London, the pieces channel a
certain 1950s-inspired *joie de vivre*. Set's specialists can
also take on projects from the design and styling of a
space to the crafting of bespoke furniture.
set.gr

ZAIRA COLLECTION
Chania, Crete

For those relocating to Crete or decking out their holiday residence, the first port of call should be Zaira, a knowledgeable purveyor of high-end furniture and accessories near the Venetian old town of Chania. Run by Evaggelia Liokoura and her daughter Zaira, the business is also a manufacturer, with a family-owned factory in Indonesia, where it makes elegant pieces from teak, suar wood and rattan. Zaira often works with international designers on bespoke furniture collections, and has delivered projects all over the world. "A big part of our clientele consists of people who have their summer homes here in Crete," says Liokoura.
zairacollection.gr

2ND FLOOR
Thessaloniki

Owner Tolis Koumparos named his business after the second floor of an industrial building where he got started in 2007. Since then, his enterprise has grown to include a bricks-and-mortar shop, showroom and a design hotel named The Trilogy House, with another one now in the works. "We mainly represent international brands for the Greek market," says Koumparos, a Thessaloniki native. "Our portfolio includes Tom Dixon, Gebrüder Thonet, Vitra, Hay, Fritz Hansen, Ferm Living, Alessi and others." What's more, 2nd Floor also provides interior design services and collaborates with architects on domestic and commercial spaces.
2ndfloor.gr

In any new environment you will need to find like-minded contacts
and collaborators and establish yourself in the community.
How better to do this than to join a club?

BUILD A NETWORK

VOULIAGMENI NAUTICAL CLUB
Athens

The red, blue and white crest of the Vouliagmeni
Nautical Club is synonymous with Olympic excellence
in Greece. Founded by local sportsmen in the 1930s,
the club has been training multiple generations of
Greek athletes, including many of its biggest names
in windsurfing and water polo. Its facilities include
a marina, a waterskiing school, junior and Olympic
competition sailing boats, an open-air swimming pool
and a gym overlooking the bay off Mikro Kavouri
peninsula. To wind down after your physical exertions,
the club's two rocky beaches, lounges and upscale
restaurant will be just what you need.
nov.gr

SPORTS CLUB
TATOÏ CLUB
Athens

Nestled beyond Athens' bustle in the northern suburb of Acharnes, Tatoï Club occupies a single-storey building currently being redesigned by Kois Architecture. This private members' club, founded in 2012, has 15 tennis courts and two for padel, state-of-the-art fitness facilities and an expert team of trainers. Landscape practice H Pangalou & Associates has overseen the grounds. "What makes us special is our proximity to nature," says the club's CEO Elli Vizantiou. To reward your efforts, there's also a spa and two pools – as well as a restaurant and activities from food classes to running, book and theatre groups that are perfect for making new friends. *tatoiclub.com*

You know where to move to, the contacts to call on and what your home is going to look like – it's time to hear from others who have chosen the country as a home for their new ventures.

SUCCESS STORIES

WINEMAKER
JÉRÔME BINDA
Tinos

French winemaker Jérôme Binda worked in Paris as an art dealer and graphic designer before settling on Tinos with his wife in 2011. After finding an ignored plot of land and seeing an opportunity to develop small-batch wines from native koumariano and mavro potamisi grapes, he decided to pursue the agricultural interests he discovered growing up in the French countryside. "I'm very moved by the craft," he says. Binda found a more suitable rhythm among Tinos' rugged surroundings. "Tinos' landscape has maintained a balance similar to how it was thousands of years ago," says Binda. "Nobody else was professionally interested in these vintage vines, but earth like this is what keeps this island interesting."

WRITER
RANA HADDAD
Athens

GALLERIST
SIMONE PIERMARIA
Syros

Italian gallerist Simone Piermaria worked in Venice, Milan, Bratislava and Basel before establishing Un Gramme gallery in Ermoupolis on Syros in early 2024. "There's something very special about this small, unstuffy port city in the heart of the Mediterranean," says Piermaria. In his adopted home, Piermaria has been studying Greek and found a particular penchant for incorporating stone and marble in his own artistic practice. "There's a refreshing rural simplicity about the island," says Piermaria. At Un Gramme, Piermaria has created an exhibition space and plays host to artists and gallerists such as Bosnian Safet Zec and Naxos-based sculptor Ingbert Brunk.

"I find Athens' architecture beautiful," says Rana Haddad, a Syrian-British novelist who settled in the Greek capital in 2018 after 22 years in London. "It's the mix of the buildings, trees and the hills. Flowers grow where they want." For Haddad, the city provides a balance between urban life and the countryside, which reminds her of Crete, where she first started spending stints in the country. She's found Athens' informality allows eccentricity to thrive and odd scenarios to occur; a coffee that becomes an all-night dinner or a performance artist sharing a stairwell with a religious grandmother. Athens's multiplicities inspired Haddad to start her own writers' salons and she is also writing her second novel.

PART 03

ADDRESS BOOK

Take a tour of the country's best hospitality,
design, culture and architecture – plus the coasts,
peaks and places not to be missed.

ATHENS

The buzzy Greek capital is laden with culture: from the marble that makes up the Parthenon on the Acropolis to the flavours of family-run tavernas and the pride of the Made in Greece label. Here's our extended list of must-visits to soak up everything this ancient metropolis has to offer.

STAY

HOTEL GRANDE BRETAGNE
Kolonaki
Originally built in 1842 as a wealthy businessman's mansion, this elegant five-star hotel on Syntagma Square is a historic Athenian institution.
marriott.com

APOLLO PALM
Psyrri
The Apollo Palm is among Athens' recent flourishing of smart downtown hotels. The 48-key stopover is housed in a 1930s former police station revamped by opera set designer Mariette Sans-Rival.
apollopalmhotel.com

SHILA
Kolonaki
A 1920s bohemian bolthole with six decorated suites ranging from rustic to artistic. Each offers either a private garden or balcony.
shila-athens.com

FOUR SEASONS ASTIR PALACE
Vouliagmeni
This luxurious beach resort offers the best of the Athenian Riviera a half-hour drive from the city centre.
fourseasons.com

KING GEORGE HOTEL
Syntagma
Traditional elegance, decor and service make this century-old establishment a firm favourite.
marriott.com

EAT & DRINK

GALLINA
Koukaki
Lovers of comfort food looking for a fine-dining spin would do well to visit here. Patrons can perch themselves on custom-designed furniture while admiring the modern art adorning the walls.
gallina.gr

Taverna ton Filon, Athens

CAFÉ AVISSINIA
Monastiraki
A cabinet of curiosities awaits in this classic Athenian stop-in on Avissinias Square. Sundays spent wandering around the antique-market stalls and shops and savouring *mezedes* with a side of ouzo are what dreams are made of.
cafeavissinia.net

LINOU SOUMPASIS K SIA
Psyrri
This modern-day greek taverna plates up a myriad of local foods in accordance with a fresh, seasonal menu perpetually in flux.
linousoumpasis.gr

FITA
Neos Kosmos
A hip restaurant with a laid-back atmosphere and a modern twist on Greek seafood classics.
+30 21 1414 8624

TAVERNA TON FILON
Kolonos
An old-school taverna with dim lights, centuries-old jasmine plants and fresh, seasonal produce delivered from local markets.
Argous 66, Athina

AKTI
Vouliagmeni
This waterside location evokes carefree summers with a Greek vibrancy that comes alive at dusk.
aktirestaurant.com

AKRA
Pangrati
Star chef Yannis Loukakis' first outpost in the Greek capital, serving dishes cooked over an open fire in the centre of the dining room.
+30 21 0725 1116

WINE IS FINE
Panepistimio
A short walk from the municipal market in downtown Athens, Wine is Fine is a relaxed wine bar-cum-bistro with chef residencies.
wineisfine.gr

KORA BAKERY
Kolonaki
A sourdough and viennoiserie bakery selling delicious rye cinnamon rolls and sourdough bread baked with the finest ingredients on the market.
korabakery.com

AFOI ASIMAKOPOULOI
Exarchia
A historic bakery and ice-cream parlour, famous for its almond *kourabiedes* cookies traditionally eaten at Christmas.
asimakopouloi.com

ANANA
Panepistimio
A bright and colourful Sixties-inspired coffee shop in the historic centre, serving cold brews, great snacks and vegan brunch dishes.
Praxitelous 33, Athina

PAPAGIANNAKOS
Mesogeia
This winery specialises in cultivating indigenous grapes – and has done so since 1919.
papagiannakos.gr

MATERIA PRIMA
Koukaki
This wine-bistro was named after the essence of the process, from the soil to the vines.
materiaprima.gr

GALAXY
Akadimia
Opened in 1972 and one of the oldest bars in Athens. It was originally decorated by a set and costume designer and has barely changed since.
Stadiou 10, Athina

DAPHNIS AND CHLOE
Neos Kosmos
This herbs and spices shop inspired by the flavours of the Mediterranean is the ideal spot to grab a fresh bouquet of oregano.
daphnisandchloe.com

PALEO WINE STORE
Piraeus
A renovated warehouse transformed into a wine shop, bar and restaurant by sommelier Yiannis Kaimenakis.
+30 21 0412 5204

VARVAKIOS FISH MARKET
Monastiraki
Named after the famous gentleman pirate Ioannis Varvakis, this fish market is the best place to buy the catch of the day.
Athinas 42, Athina

EXARCHIA FARMERS' MARKET
Exarchia
Once known as the anarchist neighbourhood of Athens, Exarchia has retained its edgy character.
Kallidromiou, Athina

TATOÏ CLUB
Acharnes
A haven of peace not far from the city, this members' club is the ideal location to reconnect with nature.
tatoiclub.com

Stallholders at Exarchia market

TANPOPO
Panepistimiou
For those times when only ramen will do, this place offers a great bowl of the Japanese noodle soup.
tanpopo.gr

SHOP
___
SET
Pikermi
A family-owned furniture company with four decades of expertise in interior design combining traditional crafts from around the world for its pieces.
set.gr

BOX INTERIORS
Kolonaki
A sleek store offering interior design and decor brands for residential and corporate spaces.
boxinteriors.gr

ANTHOLOGIST
Vathis
The secret spot of Greek design aficionados looking for unique pieces is part showroom, part event space and part exhibition gallery.
anthologist.com

PARAPHERNALIA
City Centre
Lifestyle store founded in 2014 to build a hub for creatives in the heart of the city.
paraphernalia.gr

THE NAXOS APOTHECARY
City Centre
Luxury natural fragrance and personal-care brand.
thenaxosapothecary.com

KOPRIA
Exarchia
A friendly team and a wide-ranging selection of plants, flowers, gardening tools and ceramics.
Eresou 30, Athina

CALLISTA
Kolonaki
A single leather bag, handcrafted by the skilled craftwomen of this female-founded brand, is made using 950 stitches and 356 knots.
callista.com

ANCIENT GREEK SANDALS
Monastiraki
Handmade leather sandals echoing the ancient myth of the Cretan shoemaker who made the gods' magical pairs.
ancient-greek-sandals.com

SAVAPILE
Psyrri
Savapile's handmade straw hats have adorned heads in Athens since 1960.
Agias Eleousis 14, Athina

OLGIANNA MELISSINOS SANDALS
Makrygianni
Some of the best made-to-measure leather sandals, created by owner Olgianna Melissinos.
melissinos-sandals.com

ILEANA MAKRI
Kolonaki
Ileana Makri travelled the world to find inspiration for the jewellery of her eponymous studio.
ileanamakri.com

ZEUS & DIONE
Kolonaki
A stylish lifestyle brand named after the parents of Aphrodite, the ancient Greek goddess of love and beauty.
zeusndione.com

IT'S A SHIRT
Exarchia
A clothing company with an ethos of timeless elegance created using natural dying processes and unusual textures.
itsashirt.gr

MOUKI MOU
Plaka
This shop offers a sophisticated selection of high-quality contemporary clothing, accessories, jewellery and beauty products for women and men.
moukimouathens.com

CHRISTAKIS
Akadimia and Kifisia
The Nyflis family has run this menswear shop since 1947 and continues the family legacy by making bespoke shirts and suits.
christakisathens.com

MOHXA
Kolonaki
A sunny, surf-inspired menswear and accessories company that uses retro deadstock textiles.
mohxa.com

APHILO
Kolonaki
This elegant concept store offers clothes, accessories and artworks by up-and-coming makers and artisans.
aphiloathens.com

Floral refinements on offer at Phaon

PHAON
Kolonaki
Dimitra Marlanti and Alexandros Kalogiros moved back to Athens from Italy to open a sophisticated store that sells elegant fragrances and fresh flowers.
phaon-athens.com

CRINI AND SOPHIA
Quality home-grown goods for the table from textiles to ceramics and glassware in both contemporary and traditional designs for all manner of hosting styles.
criniandsophia.com

IOAM APOTHEKE
Gazi
Connect with the scents, textures and flavours of Crete through the soothing homeware and skincare products from this company which is inspired by the island and its many artisans.
10amapotheke.com

HYPER HYPO
Monastiraki
Hyper Hypo opened in 2021 to create a meeting point for the city's art and design scene. Head to the shop for the best art books and magazines by local talent, plus international titles.
hyperhypo.gr

ADAD BOOKS
Petralona
Adad is a bookshop-cum-café founded by Belgian curator Alix Janta-Polczynski. The go-to spot for bookworms and coffee-lovers (or wine if you fancy) provides a laid-back atmosphere in keeping with the Petralona neighbourhood.
Anteou 1, Athens

DO

MUSEUM OF CYCLADIC ART
Kolonaki
A collection of Cycladic and ancient Greek art, including marble figurines, jewellery, vases and other objects from the Archaic, Classical and Byzantine eras.
cycladic.gr

NATIONAL ARCHAEOLOGICAL MUSEUM
Exarchia
The largest museum in Greece was built in the 19th century and hosts thousands of treasures from archaeological sites nationwide.
namuseum.gr

NATIONAL MUSEUM OF CONTEMPORARY ART (EMST)
Koukaki
Established in 2000 in a former brewery, EMST celebrates contemporary artists from Greece and around the world.
emst.gr

SYLVIA KOUVALI
Piraeus
Found a short walk away from the port, this gallery was one of the first to set up in Piraeus and is younger sister to the successful gallery of the same name in Soho, London.
sylviakouvali.com

GOULANDRIS MUSEUM OF CONTEMPORARY ART
Pangrati
This five-storey art museum in a renovated 1920s mansion displays paintings, sculptures furniture and more.
goulandris.gr

ENTROPIA
Agios Panteleimonas
This record store, filled with titles from contemporary artists and traditional music, was created by two friends in 2017.
entropia-records.com

ALEKOS FASSIANOS MUSEUM
Metaxourgeio
A museum dedicated to the eponymous artist within his former family home. The interior design was carefully chosen to best display his work and legacy.
alekosfassianos.gr

NATIONAL GALLERY – ALEXANDROS SOUTSOS MUSEUM
Pangrati
The most important museum about Greece's artistic history can be found just a few steps away from Syntagma Square.
nationalgallery.gr

MEGARON ATHENS CONCERT HALL
Kolonaki
Opened in 1991, the Megaron Athens Concert Hall has established itself as a cultural hub at the centre of Athens' cultural scene, offering opera and concerts in one of the best acoustic halls in Europe.
megaron.gr

Contemplation at Vorres Museum

THE BREEDER
Metaxourgio
This art gallery in Athens was founded by Stathis Panagoulis and George Vamvakidis as an extension of the magazine of the same name.
thebreedersystem.com

THE INTERMISSION
Pireas
Since 2019 Intermission has been providing both new and established artists from Greece and beyond with a flexible space for site-specific installations and exhibitions.
theintermission.art

UNDERFLOW
Koukaki
South of the Acropolis, this distinctive space is a record store, bar, live stage and art gallery all wrapped up into one. The varied vinyl selection makes this a must for record lovers.
underflow.gr

VORRES MUSEUM
Paiania
Housed in a 19th-century house in the Athenian suburbs, this museum contains a personal collection of historical Greek objects assembled by art historian Ian Vorres.
vorresmuseum.gr

VOULIAGMENI NAUTICAL CLUB
Vouliagmeni
Founded by local sportsmen in 1937 in the seaside resort of Vouliagmeni, this club is complete with a marina, members' lounges and Olympic competition sailing boats.
nov.gr

BENAKI MUSEUM GIKA GALLERY
Kolonaki
Inside a modernist building by renowned architect Konstantinos Kitsikis are some of the major works by influential 20th-century Greek painter Nikos Hadjikyriakos-Ghikas.
benaki.org

BIOS
Monastiraki
An arts and performance venue with a difference, in the form of a cool rooftop bar with incredible views of the Acropolis
pireos84.bios.gr

ILIAS LALAOUNIS JEWELRY MUSEUM
Acropoli
The first museum devoted to the art of jewellery with an impressive permanent collection.
lalaounis.com

ATHENS

THE ADDRESS BOOK

CRETE

Crete is Greece's largest and most populated island. With a rich and ancient history, the promise of beautiful hotels, a strong community of artisans and plenty of splendid culinary experiences, there are many reasons to visit this Mediterranean hideaway. This list provides just a few of them.

STAY

AMMOS
Chania
A crisp, modernist take on white-walled Greek tradition, Ammos features cool and relaxing rooms, excellent food, a pool and beach access.
ammoshotel.com

METOHI KINDELIS
Chania
These three guest houses are surrounded by avocado orchards and each feature their own private pool, patio and gardens.
metohi-kindelis.gr

PHAEA BLUE PALACE
Elounda
With a choice of serene private bungalows and suites, this hotel combines elevated surroundings with casual and smart dining opportunities for all moods, including authentic home-cooked Greek feasts on a communal table set in the gardens on the property.
bluepalace.gr

ELOR HOUSE
Chania
Available to hire year-round, this small, restored townhouse is the perfect base from which to explore Chania on foot before heading out on wider Cretan adventures on four wheels.
Thrakis 3

EAT & DRINK

HASIKA
Rethymno
Since opening in 2018, chef Michalis Chasikos has made a name for himself by taking classic Greek dishes – the likes of the Greek salad and *spanakopita* – and adding a modern twist.
hasika.gr

Shaded terrace at the Ammos hotel

THALASSINO AGERI
Chania
This taverna serves seafood dishes on tables right beside the harbour, making it the perfect spot for a sunset dinner.
thalasino-ageri.gr

LYRARAKIS
Heraklion
Producing Cretan wines including malvasia, liatiko and kotsifali; Lyrarakis is bringing back ancient grape varieties from the brink of extinction. The mandilari red tastes like succulent cherry pie in a bottle.
lyrarakis.com

PESKESI
Heraklion
Hidden within a narrow passageway in the old cobbled city of Heraklion, Peskesi offers traditional Cretan cuisine with a farm-to-table ethos.
peskesicrete.gr

ALEKOS
Rethymno
This classic village taverna offers Cretan meat-based dishes with a set menu and cosy atmosphere with stone walls and wooden tables.
+30 28 3104 1185

RED JANE
Chania
Housed in an old foundry, this bakery has gained popularity for its minimalist marble design as well as its breads and sweets.
redjane.com

THEORIST
Rethymno
This breezy café-cum-library has a touch of Scandi minimalism and is a favourite of Rethymno locals for its great coffee and brunch.
theorist.livemenu.gr

NERO
Spili
Each product in this deli and produce store is chosen for its branding design and aesthetic packaging. Items available range from olive oil to tea, chocolate to sea salt.
+30 69 3658 0419

35N
Sfakaki
On the outskirts of Rethymno, 35N distillery produces *tsikoudia*, a fiery spirit made using grape remnants from the winemaking process that has been enjoyed here since the Ottoman occupation. The *tsikoudia* made with thyme honey makes a perfect digestif after a *meze* feast.
35n.gr

MAIAMI
Chania
When artist Alexandra Manousakis moved from New York to Chania, a little art-deco building near the main harbour stole her heart. The building still features salmon-pink doors and windows and is now an art gallery and brasserie all in one, serving dishes on Manousakis' own ceramic creations.
maiamichania.com

ILIANA MALIHIN WINERY
Melampes
One of the most talked about young wine-makers in Greece, Iliana Malihin makes organic red, white and rosé wines from her elevated mountain vineyards.
+30 69 7934 4044

ELAIA
Kapsaliana
Within the Kapsaliana Hotel, this fine-dining experience offers Cretan and Mediterranean recipes with a modern twist.
kapsalianavillage.gr

SHOP

STAGAKIS CRETAN LYRA
Rethymno
Each wall of this shop features handmade instruments on display, from the traditional Cretan lyra to mandolins and lutes, many of them shaped from reclaimed wood from old local buildings.
stagakis-manolis.gr

EA CERAMICS
Margarites
A contemporary interpretation of ancient Greek pottery styles, EA Ceramics was established in 2010 to create sculptural earthenware for the home.
eaceramicstudio.com

CARMELA IATROPOULOU
Chania
Carmela Iatropoulou's small, perfectly appointed jewellery and ceramics store provides a corner of calm. It is situated a short distance from the port, where small windows, low light and unique pieces made by local craftspeople lend the place a sacred energy.
Aggelou 7

Uncorking at Metohi Kindelis

JUSTBRAZIL
Chania
Justbrazil is São Paulo native Renata Leitao's clothing and accessories shop featuring sleek pleats, silk scarves and statement jewellery. Her little empire extends from here to Mykonos and speaks to long, luxe summers, even when there's a little nip in the air.
justbrazilstore.gr

ARCHAETYPON
Heraklion
Architect Maria Schoinaraki and architectural technician Evangelos Tzanopoulos joined forces in 2020 to create this interiors and lifestyle concept store.
archaetypon.gr

CRETAN KNIVES SKALIDAKIS
Chania
Cretan Knives Skalidakis makes, sells and sharpens everything from Samurai-style blades to butcher's meat cleavers.
cretanknives.gr

DO

HERAKLION ARCHAEOLOGICAL MUSEUM
Heraklion
One of Europe's finest, this museum contains objects covering 5,500 years of history, from the Neolithic era to Roman times.
heraklionmuseum.gr

MUSEUM OF CONTEMPORARY ART OF CRETE
Rethymno
It's only natural that the Museum of Contemporary Art of Crete would be located in one of the island's first industrial spaces. This old Venetian building used to be a soap factory. The 1,000 sq m space was acquired then turned into a gallery in 1995, and is now home to over 700 works by Greek artists from 1950 to today.
cca.gr

MUNICIPAL ART GALLERY OF CHANIA
Chania
Hosting paintings, engravings and sculpture dating back to the 18th century in a historic building in the centre of the city.
pinakothiki-chania.gr

CYCLADES

At the centre of the Aegean, the Cyclades comprises around 220 islands. It's safe to say there won't be a shortage of things to do and see when you visit. Here's our round-up of the best beachside boltholes and romantic restaurants, where you'll be greeted with warm hospitality.

STAY

THE ROOSTER
Antiparos
The "retreat" meets the "resort" at this roost. Relax in an intimate and carefree environment at the heart of this tiny jewel of an island in the southern Aegean.
theroosterantiparos.com

MÈLISSES
Andros
With a name meaning "bees", Mèlisses is a secluded gastronomic homestay hosted by Italian-born Allegra Pomilio on the island of Andros, where animals roam freely and the food is grown fresh nearby.
melissesandros.com

BELVEDERE
Mykonos
The best views of the Aegean and Mykonos' vibrant social scene can both be found within the elegant grounds of this hotel run by the Ioannidis family.
belvederehotel.com

GUNDARI
Folegandros
A luxury resort within a rugged, rocky landscape. The site's design – pieced together by Athens' acclaimed studio Block722 – takes its cues from the natural tones of the island.
gundari.com

ISTORIA
Santorini
This Santorini boutique stay is in the southeast of the island, overlooking black-sand beaches contrasting with the blue Aegean Sea. Istoria is the embodiment of exquisite and thoughtfully luxurious hospitality.
istoriahotel.gr

Inquisitive Cycladian goats

VERINA ASTRA
Sifnos
Spacious and stylish coastal accommodation, with private verandas offering a view out and over the Aegean.
verinahotelsifnos.com

PARILIO
Paros
Designed by Athens-based interior design company Laboratorium, this 33-suite hotel – with its white walls and clean-lined furniture – fully emphasises the elegance of Cycladic architecture.
par+iliohotelparos.com

ARGINI
Syros
Established in a refurbished mansion dating back to 1853, this marble-laden 12-key hotel is marked as part of Hermoupolis's cultural heritage.
arginisyros.gr

ARISTIDE
Syros
In a luxurious mansion, Aristide hosts nine distinctly different suites, an art gallery with an artist residence and two bars. For holidaymakers looking for elegance.
hotelaristide.com

KTIMA LEMONIES
Andros
This 200-year-old farm surrounded by lemon groves was turned into a five-key guesthouse in harmony with the island's rhythm of life.
ktimalemonies.gr

SKINOPI LODGE
Milos
This nine-acre property houses seven stone villas on a slope looking over the sea. With open-fronted accommodation, the sea breeze – and a natural serenity – drifts in.
skinopi.com

THE WILD
Mykonos
This creatively designed hotel reflects the penchant for interiors and design of founder Nikos Varveris – also founder of Greek interiors retailer Moda Bagno.
thewildhotel.com

DEOS
Mykonos
A 10-minute stroll from Mykonos Town, Deos is a 42-key hotel on a hill overlooking the old harbour. Designed by Galal Mahmoud of Beirut-based GM Architects, the whitewashed buildings sits among gardens with silver olive trees and large terracotta amphorae.
deosmykonos.gr

EAT & DRINK

CANTINA
Sifnos
The cantina in this restaurant's name is a small cellar and pantry used to ferment, cure and dry produce for its menu. There's a bohemian, laid-back terrace overlooking the bay, below the medieval citadel of Kastro.
cantinasifnos.gr

PAPAIOANNOU
Mykonos
A restaurant for fish lovers. Lolling over the relaxed Agios Stefanos beach, you can watch beachgoers from the outdoor terrace, and see where your food has come from.
papaioannou-restaurants.com

RIZES
Mykonos
Self-proclaimed folkloric farmstead hosted by a Mykonian family in a lush natural setting. A homestay giving a taste of another way of life.
rizesmykonos.com

CASA FISTIKI
Antiparos
Situated by the sea in Agios Georgios, this Mexican-Mediterranean establishment serves a refined menu of delicious dishes, as well as a beach take-away service.
casafistiki.com

BOUNTARAKI
Paros
Right by Paros's port, this little taverna serves up great plates to locals and tourists alike. Order a bottle of wine and a moussaka while enjoying the sounds of the sea.
+30 22 8402 2297

TO THALASSAKI
Tinos
Found on the bay of Ysternia, this restaurant – literally on the beach – offers creative and aromatic cuisine and a rich wine list.
+30 22 8303 1366

ESTATE ARGYROS
Santorini
An artisanal island winery that specialises in small-batch wines that are big on quality. With a rolling roster of three cuvées, each sold on allocation, you're guaranteed concentration and complexity.
estateargyros.com

The view at 180° Sunset Bar

TERÉZA
Tinos
This café is uniquely set up inside a grocery store and spills out invitingly into a courtyard, offering a colourful interior and many traditional Greek favourites.
+30 2283 041320

FOKOS TAVERNA
Mykonos
A simple building with a lovely view of the bay and the hills that tumble down towards it. The perfect place to enjoy a beer and some food, served family-style away from the crowds.
fokostavernamykonos.com

CHERONISSOS FISH TAVERN
Sifnos
Few taverns can offer such an authentically relaxed vibe. With a menu inevitably packed full of seafood dishes, this tavern overlooks the picturesque bay below.
+30 22 8403 3119

DRAKOS TAVERNA
Ios
On the end of Mylopotas beach, this tavern on the pier serves seafood fresh from the boat, under glowing orange lamplight. Try the lobster.
drakostaverna.com

DJANGO GELATO
Syros
A gelateria serving handmade ice creams and sorbets from fresh, local ingredients, with zero waste. The perfect pick-me-up for hot Syros summers.
djangogelato.com

EPTA
Syros
A breakfast spot off the main square, easily recognisable due to its elegant glass doorway, high ceilings and exposed brick with marble slabs.
Peloponnisou 7, Ermoupoli

180° SUNSET BAR
Mykonos
Set on a large stone terrace, Mykonos' supreme sunset spot offers an ambient, panoramic view to enjoy a cocktail at the end of a long day spent enjoying the island.
180.bar

SIMÁ
Tinos
This funky restaurant is characterised by its goat logo. The real goat who inspired the logo, called "Jo", goes out of her way to pursue the finest and freshest that the local area offers, just like Simá's owner-restaurateurs.
simatinos.com

CYCLADES

THE ADDRESS BOOK

LOGGIA WINE BAR
Sifnos
With the tagline "wine from a rock", it's clear the Loggia bar crew like to keep things simple. Great wine, views and tapas, served atop a rock, in Kastro, Sifnos.
Kastro 84003

TO MELISSI
Paros
A small, family-run deli that highlights Parian gastronomy, as well as Cycladic wine, cheese and dried goods.
+30 22 8405 5377

CANTINA ANALOGUE
Syros
A natural-wine bar, designed by a Cyclades-native artist, that encourages foodies and art lovers to come and try its expansive food menu – or attend a movie night.
+30 22 8130 2412

BARDÓT
Antiparos
Design studio Manhattan Project paired terracotta tones with dimpled white limestone in a modern blend with the island's old-world glamour.
+30 22 8406 3072

MAKRYONITIS SYROS DISTILLERY
Syros
This microdistillery launched in 2017 to distil native Cycladian grape pomace. The first to produce distillate from fresh Syros figs, it uses a slow distillation process to make traditional Greek spirits such as ouzo and *mastiha*.
syrosdistillery.gr

ALEMAGOU BEACH CLUB
Mykonos
Enjoy the view from your own cabana or beach lounge and follow up with cockails in the sunset lounge. Everything you need for a day – and an evening – at the beach.
alemagou.gr

SHOP

ANTILALOS
Tinos
A bookstore, café and bar all in one, occasionally hosting events, Antilalos also offers a rich selection of second-hand editions arranged on shelving throughout the three-story store.
+30 22 8302 6488

Clifftop chapel, Folegandros

MAISON STAMATA
Tinos
This eclectic concept boutique with its blue and white-striped ceiling and terazzo flooring sells everything from clothing to accessories and homewares, all in bright colours.
+30 22 8302 3503

MAISON BARDÓT
Antiparos
Established in a 17th-century shipbuilder's house, this art gallery – a traditionally crafted, stucco-walled affair – is an island cultural hub.
Pounta, Antiparos 840 07

TAXIDI
Tinos
A multifunctional location set in a converted 1930s property, including a café, gallery and shop space.
taxiditinos.com

MORETHANTHIS
Antiparos
Jewellery shop offering a range of pieces from both Greek and international designers.
morethanthis.gr

MOTIF
Syros
A dainty, naturally lit shop space selling hand-crafted fine ceramics. The product range principally takes cues from Cycladic motifs.
motifdesign.gr

YANNIS SERGAKIS
Paros
A prominent purveyor of diamond jewellery, each piece is made in a traditional workshop by artisans with a deep knowledge in the trade.
yannissergakis.com

CHIMERA
Syros
Behind the Apollon theatre this multifaceted space sells jewellery, paintings, sculptures and tapestry.
chimeracraft.gr

AESTHET
Mykonos
Offering primarily beachwear and resortwear, this luxury boutique can be found in the heart of cosmopolitan Nammos Village.
aesthet.com

MAAN
Antiparos
Marilena Andreadi founded her brand in 2015, making swimsuits that echo the slow lifestyle of the Greek islands.
maanislandwear.com

PARTHENIS
Mykonos
A clothing brand with minimal, classic designs with a focus on craftsmanship, which has been operating since the 1970s.
orsalia-parthenis.gr

ZOSMA
Tinos
A concept store in a historic building formerly occupied by a candle-making atelier that had been operated by an orthodox priest.
Leof. Megalocharis 31, Tinos 842 00

NÉ EN AOÛT
Mykonos
The name may mean "Born in August" in French, but "Né en Août" is a proud Mykonos menswear brand that embraces a minimal aesthetic fit for all months of the year.
neenaout.com

WAIKIKI
Andros
A local label and concept store based in Chora, Andros' capital. The line of products is driven particularly by collaborations with talented young designers.
Andros 845 00

NIKOS KOULIS
Mykonos
Established in 2006, Nikos Koulis' has fine jewellery ateliers in Athens, Mykonos and Paros. His Cycladic designs are well-known for their delicacy and use of precious stones.
nikoskoulis.com

ZEYELO
Syros
Inspired by their native Mediterranean climate, designers Eleni Vakondiou and Periklis Therrios founded Zeyelo, an eyewear brand which creates glasses with wooden frames lacquered with a beeswax and olive oil concoction.
zeyelo.com

DO

MUSEUM OF CONTEMPORARY ART (MOCA)
Andros
Looking out over the Aegean Sea, this art gallery owned by the Goulandris Foundation hosts all manner of Cycladic art, as well as names of global renown, including Rodin, Giacometti and Picasso.
goulandris.gr

Boats in Naoussa harbour, Paros

TOMATO INDUSTRIAL MUSEUM
Santorini
Once an old tomato factory that was part of a wider operation that produced and processed the famously small Santorini tomatoes that are used for making tomato paste. The museum was established in 2014 to provide insight on the cultivation, production and processing of the fruit.
tomatomuseum.gr

LA CHAPELLE SAINT-ANTOINE
Naxos
After falling in love with this old 17th-century monastery, a French family transformed it into an artist's residency, opening the doors to a breathtaking architectural edifice at the heart of Kastro.
lachapellesaintantoine.com

YANNOULIS HALEPAS MUSEUM
Tinos
Yannoulis Halepas' house was turned into a museum to honour the sculptor's work. An iconic figure of Greek modern art, his home still breathes creativity and artistry.
Pyrgos 842 01

UN GRAMME
Syros
Un Gramme is a unique non-profit organisation that offers a space for artists, gallerists, curators and institutions to showcase pioneering projects. A place for audacious, independent figures.
ungramme.org

THERMIA PROJECT
Kythnos
An art residency dedicated to supporting community engagement, while encouraging artists to incorporate local traditions into their own contemporary vision.
thermiaproject.com

ALEKOS FASSIANOS ATELIER
Kea
Overlooking the Aegean, this white-washed building is the former home and atelier of the late Greek artist Alekos Fassianos. The artist's work is visible throughout the building, from metal railings depicting a man's profile to handmade personal items.
alekosfassianos.gr

CYCLADES

THE ADDRESS BOOK

DODECANESE

The Dodecanese, consisting of more than 160 islands dotted across the southeastern Aegean and curving towards Turkey, have a deep link to antiquity and a reputation for beautiful beaches. Across Rhodes, Kos, Leros and more, ancient sites await visitors to these sun-soaked island gems.

STAY

LINDOS VILLAS
Rhodes
The estate comprises three villas in an ancient fishing village on the shores of the Aegean, including a 16th-century sea captain's house.
lindos-villas.com

MEDITERRANEO
Kastellorizo
This hotel is in an 18th-century building on the shore overlooking Turkey. Guests enter through a garden of flowering oleander and red geraniums.
mediterraneokastellorizo.com

ARCHONTIKO ANGELOU
Leros
Minutes from the sea, Archontiko Angelou is a little oasis of calm. This family-run bed and breakfast offers a delicious breakfast including home-made jams, fresh bread and fruit – perfect for a relaxing break.
hotel-angelou-leros.com

PAGOSTAS
Patmos
Renowned landscape architect Helli Pangalou and designer Leda Athanasopoulou helped the founders put a minimalist spin on this traditional Greek guesthouse.
pagostas.com

OKU HOTEL
Kos
With a name derived from Japanese spiritual concepts of inner space, Oku champions laid-back luxury.
okuhotels.com

CASA COOK RHODES
Kolymbia
Disarmingly relaxed and gracious environment with neutral, natural tactile furnishings and finishes.
casacook.com

Lemons at Archontiko Angelou

EAT & DRINK

DILAILA
Lipsi
This bar and restaurant sports one of the best views of Katsadia beach. Order the feta and orange salad.
+30 22 4704 1041

CÉSAR MEZE BAR
Rhodes
This fine dining *meze* bar in the heart of Lindos has earned its prestigious Greek Cuisine Award by reinventing Greek dishes like the tuna gyros with anchovy cream, tomato chutney, marinated onion and seaweed.
caesarslindos.com

ÉLA
Patmos
Éla's dedication to regenerating the island's fertile soil and the farm-to-table approach shows an admiration for Patmian agricultural traditions. Enjoy grilled sea bass and fresh gazpacho made with Éla's homegrown produce.
ela.wine

KYMA
Patmos
A seafood restaurant with one of the most dramatic dine-with-a-view experiences in Greece, Kyma serves traditional dishes while guests enjoy the sun setting over Chora, the island's capital, and the Monastery of Patmos.
Aspri Patmou

MELISSA HONEY FACTORY
Kos
This honey workshop was founded in 2009 on the west side of the island by the Drosos family, which has been involved in the honey business for over a century.
+30 22 4207 2260

DO

KAPOPOULOS FINE ARTS
Patmos
Founded in 1991, this art gallery is at the forefront of the modern art scene in Greece. It opened its space in the capital Chora in 2015 to promote new and established artists from around the Dodecanese.
kapopoulosfinearts.com

MUSEUM OF MODERN GREEK ART OF RHODES
Rhodes
Spread over four showrooms, this museum specialises in collecting 20th-century Greek masterpieces, such as painter Spero Vassiliou's "Clean Monday Feast".
mgamuseum.gr

IONIAN ISLANDS

Known for their verdant landscapes, the Ionian islands stretch from Corfu in the north to Cythera in the south, covering most of the western Peloponnese coast. Book a stay at one of the restorative retreats on these diverse islands, or shop at one of the many artisan workshops.

STAY

F ZEEN
Kefalonia
A luxurious adults-only retreat that aims to leave you spiritually nourished physically restored in a beautiful Kefalonian landscape.
fzeenretreats.com

THE PELIGONI CLUB
Zakynthos
Small but mighty, this family-run island beachclub and villa holiday location is designed for a combination of swimming and sunbathing.
peligoni.com

DOMES OF CORFU
Corfu
Overlooked by tree-covered mountains, this lush beachfront hotel has four unique locations for fine-dining.
domesresorts.com

EAT & DRINK

CAKE BOUTIQUE
Corfu
As the name suggests, the confectionery offered here is made with flavour and artistry, including a rainbow array of award-winning macaroons.
+30 26 6102 3824

DR KAVVADIA'S ORGANIC FARM
Corfu
On the organic farm that once belonged to his doctor grandfather, Apostolos Porsanidis-Kavvadia carries on the family tradition of producing award-winning quality olive oil. Farm stays and visits, and tastings are available, for an immersive experience amongst the ancient olive groves.
drkavvadia.com

The Venetian Well, Corfu

THE VENETIAN WELL
Corfu
In a small hidden square in the town of Corfu, this romantic restaurant boasts a varied wine list and is open all year.
venetianwell.gr

SHOP

PATOUNIS
Corfu
These natural olive soaps have been made by the Patounis family since 1850 using traditional recipes, techniques and tools.
patounis.gr

MYRTO ZIRINI CERAMICS
Corfu
This ceramics workshop and showroom features pieces made by Myrto Zirini herself with smooth textures and organic design.
myrtozirini.gr

LAMPRINI CHANTZIARA
Corfu
Impressively elaborate statement jewellery using a range of unusual techniques and materials.
lamprinichantziara.com

DO

MUSEUM OF D SOLOMOS AND OTHER EMINENT PEOPLE OF ZAKYNTHOS
Zakynthos
A museum inside a neoclassical building that celebrates the life of the poet and writer of the Greek national anthem Dionysios Solomos, who is buried here among exhibits about other celebrated islanders.
zakynthos-museumsolomos.gr

MUSEUM OF ASIAN ART
Corfu
Founded in 1928, this museum champions Sino-Japanese art, with a large collection featuring around 15,000 works.
matk.gr

ACHILLION PALACE
Corfu
A breathtaking palace with an architectural style focused on motifs from Greek mythology, in particular the warrior Achilles.
achillion-corfu.gr

KORGIALENEIO HISTORICAL AND FOLKLORE MUSEUM
Kefalonia
This museum opened in 1962 and exhibits everyday items dating back to the 16th century that depict the island's social and cultural history.
+30 26 7102 8835

NORTH AEGEAN & SPORADES

Taking their name from the Greek for "scattered", the Sporades archipelago is spread across the northwest Aegean, a less-visited part of Greece. Here, we've compiled everything from the rustic ceramicists on Skyros to a restaurant under shady pines on Thassos.

STAY

AGORA RESIDENCE
Chios
Once a private residence dating back to the 1890s, this nine-key hotel retains its charming original features combined with contemporary design accents.
agoraresidence.com

EAT & DRINK

THE LOST SHEEP
Thassos
Greek haute cuisine that is served in a secret garden beneath the shade of a century-old pine tree.
aforarthotel.gr

KUBRICK BAR
Chios
A fun option at the centre of Chios dedicated to iconic American film director Stanley Kubrick. Enjoy a rum and lime cocktail watched over by a mural of the legend himself.
+30 22 7110 2744

FLOUR POWER
Lesvos
Luciano van der Toorn and Suzanne de Vries' bakery uses wild yeasts and stone-ground organic flours. On the menu each morning are country bread and fresh baguettes.
Skala Eresou

METAXA LIKNON
Samos
For millennia, the mountain slopes on the island of Samos have produced the finest muscat grapes – the key ingredient in Metaxa, the iconic Greek spirit. Liknon's award-winning visitor centre mirrors the vineyard terraces, with low-rise stepped buildings housing a bar and heritage centre.
metaxa.com

Metaxa Liknon, Samos

AGNANTI
Skopelos
With a dimly-lit veranda overlooking the sea, this restaurant offers fresh, colourful plates of slow-cooked pork shoulder with Skopelos prunes and a healthy wine list to match.
agnanti.com.gr

FALTAINA SWEETS
Skyros
Established in 1983, this award-winning confectionery specialises in traditional Skyrian almond sweets.
faltaina.com

SHOP

FTOULIS SKYRIAN CERAMICS
Skyros
Elegant and detailed hand-painted wares that utilise rich and distinct colours to depict pastoral motifs, made by a self-taught ceramicist in a workshop established in 1968.
Magazia Beach

KOUKOS DE LAB
Lesvos
Established in a village outside of Lesvos, innovative design duo Irene Moutsogianni and Christos Ververis turn bio-waste into furniture using eco-material harvested from Lesvos' extensive olive tree groves.
koukosdelab.com

DO

ART SPACE PYTHAGORION
Samos
Since 2012 this exhibition space has been enlightening Samos natives with annual summer events staged by the non-profit Schwarz Foundation.
schwarzfoundation.com

K-GOLD LESVOS
Lesvos
A contemporary art gallery based in Lesvos and travelling all over the country with exhibitions, performances and art fairs. A must-stop to discover Greece's emerging artists.
kgoldtemporarygallery.tumblr.com

DEO
Chios
As the only contemporary art establishment on Chios, Deo stands as a platform revitalising the island's cultural scene through free events and exhibitions for all.
deoprojects.com

NORTHERN GREECE

From Kalamas on the western side to Halkidiki's three-pronged peninsulas in the east, the upper half of Greece is less touristy, with varied terrain. Characterised by Balkan and Turkish influences and a capricious climate, northern Greece is an area of stunning natural beauty.

STAY

EKIES
Vourvourou
A contemporary addition to the coastal surroundings, this hotel's design blends metal and concrete with earth tones, and stone and wood finishes. The atmosphere is completed by lush gardens and the sound of cicadas.
ekies.gr

APEIROS CHORA
Zagori
Consisting of six accommodation options, this hotel occupies a traditional mansion built in the 18th century, now run by the eighth generation of the original owners.
apeiroschora.gr

GRAND FOREST METSOVO
Metsovo
Found near the picturesque village of Metsovo, this is a destination for nature lovers and those seeking excursions in pristine landscapes.
grand-forest.gr

IMARET
Kavala
In 2004, Kavalan native Anna Missirian reopened this Ottoman property as a hotel, complete with ornate Persian-style rugs from her family's collection, bronze wash basins made in Cairo, Kavalan marble and French linens.
imaret.gr

EAT & DRINK

BLACK DROP
Kavala
A modern coffee hub with a unique take on a café interior. Get your caffeine fix in a spot kitted out by Ark4lab of Architecture, who opt for exposed concrete and communal wooden slabs to recline on, alongside tall elegant stools.
Kassandrou 1

A waiter at the Squirrel, Halkidiki

MIKRO PAPIGO 1700
Papigo
Forming what appears to be its own mini village within Papigo, this hotel and spa offers privacy in a beautiful landscape.
mikropapigo.gr

PSARAKI
Kavala
Ouzo bar meets fish tavern at this delightful dock-side spot. Psaraki serves traditional Kavalan dishes alongside *meze*.
psaraki.gr

DISKO ROMEIKO
Litochoro
Wine bar and restaurant inside Enipeas gorge, featuring classic Greek dishes and live music.
+30 23 5208 2390

THE SQUIRREL
Halkidiki
Within The Danai hotel, this fine-dining restaurant has five tables and a panoramic view of the sea.
thedanai.com

NIKOS AND JULIA
Papigo
A traditional restaurant operating out of a complex of guesthouses offering quality regional food.
nikosiouliapapigo.gr

KANELA & GARYFALLO
Vitsa
Known for its mushroom dishes, this spot overlooks the Vikos gorge.
kanela-garyfallo.gr

SELECT
Ioannina
This bakery serves the best *bougatsa* (custard-filled phyllo pastry), with both sweet and savoury options.
+30 26 5107 1073

SHOP

TELIS GIANNENA
Ioannina
A purveyor of handmade household and gardening tools for more than 80 years, this quaint shop stands out in an age of mass-production.
telisgiannena.gr

DO

SILVERSMITHING MUSEUM
Ioannina
Located in the castle of Ioannina, this museum chronicles the evolution of silversmithing. The collection has a host of ornate artefacts, from jewellery to weapons.
+30 26 5106 4065

PELOPONNESE

The Peloponnese peninsula is the southernmost part of the mainland and boasts many sites from Greece's storied history. We've prepared a guide on where to stay after a day of sightseeing, so whether it's 17th-century mansions or lush olive groves, the Peloponnese is delightfully varied.

STAY

LASPI
Pefkali
The villas, named Petres (stones) and Skóni (dust), accommodate six guests each and are available to rent year-round as holiday homes.
laspi.life

DEXAMENES
Kourouta
A design-forward industrial hotel right on the seafront, which, aided by Greek architecture firm K-Studio, repurposed a derelict 1920s winery.
dexamenes.com

MANNA
Magouliana
This mountain wellness sanctuary is tucked into the ancient fir forest of Mount Mainalo and features a hammam and spa.
mannaarcadia.gr

KINSTERNA
Monemvasia
Surrounded by olive groves and vineyards with views of the Aegean Sea, this hotel occupies a 17th-century mansion in the quiet Peloponnesian countryside.
kinsternahotel.gr

OPORA
Pirgiotika
A handful of self-contained rooms and a secluded private villa built using local materials and using traditional techniques on a 40-acre farm of olive groves and orange orchards. Guests are treated to long days in the shade beside the pool and delicious homemade meals made with simple, locally-sourced organic ingredients.
oporacountryliving.com

Breakfast at Opora, Pirgiotika

AMANZOE
Agios Panteleimonas
Surrounded by olive groves and the Aegean Sea, this sprawling, luxurious hotel sits within a series of Unesco-protected ruins.
aman.com

THE BOLD TYPE
Patras
This 19th-century classic building was renovated into a five-star boutique hotel and fine dining restaurant, with touches reminiscent of its aristocratic heritage.
theboldtypehotel.com

EUMELIA
Gouves
A sustainable farm-stay where guests enjoy farm-to-table fare, as well as wine and olive oil tastings in the Greek countryside.
eumelia.com

EAT & DRINK

LELA'S TAVERNA
Kardamyli
This classic taverna serves contemporary Greek food on a terrace that overlooks the Mediterranean and that is shaded by grape vines.
lelastaverna.com

MPLE KANARINI
Kalamata
In the heart of Kalamata, Mple Kanarini chef and owner Konstantinos Vassiliadis collaborates with local farmers and fishermen to create unique dishes that change with the seasons.
+30 27 2104 3075

SHOP

ZERVOBEAKOS POTTERY
Pyrgos Dirou
Each piece on display in this spacious studio was made by Alexandros Zervobeakos and builds on centuries of Greek craftmanship.
zervobeakospottery.com

DO

LEIGH FERMOR HOUSE
Kardamyli
The house-museum of travel writer Sir Patrick Leigh Fermor is a point of pride for many Maniots, the traditional inhabitants of the Mani peninsula. The English writer found sanctuary here in the 1960s and fell in love with the area and its people.
benaki.org

SARONIC ISLANDS

As the closest archipelago to Athens, the Saronic islands are the easiest to combine with a trip to the capital. Including Hydra, Spetses and Aegina, these destinations in the Saronic Gulf provide a quick island retreat. Surrounded by crystal clear waters, Athens will seem worlds away.

STAY

NIKOLAOU RESIDENCE
Aegina
Get a glimpse into the life of painter Nikos Nikolaou by checking in at his former home.
nikolaouresidence.gr

BRATSERA
Hydra
An ancient sponge factory turned elegant boutique hotel, Bratsera is nestled in Hydra's picturesque heart.
bratserahotel.com

HOTEL LETO
Hydra
A refined 22-key retreat in the heart of Hydra, Hotel Leto has wooden furniture, cream fabrics and traditional tiled floors in the spirit of classic Hydriot mansions.
letohydra.gr

YAYAKI
Spetses
The founders returned from time spent abroad in 2021 with the ambition of opening a hotel. Guests are treated to delicious locally-sourced vegetarian breakfasts.
yayaki-spetses.com

POSEIDONION GRAND HOTEL
Spetses
Opened in 1914 on the car-free island of Spetses, over a century later this lavish property is still a favourite for city-weary Athenians.
poseidonion.com

EAT & DRINK

WINDMILL HYDRA
Hydra
If you are looking for an ideal spot on Hydra to admire the sunset, look no further. The Windmill Hydra serves delicious cocktails, named after the old windmill it occupies. A statue nearby commemorates the Sophia Loren film *Boy on a Dolphin*, which the windmill appears in.
Hydra 18040

Fishing boats off Hydra

TECHNE
Hydra
Opened in 2016 by Jason Barios and Yannis Michalopoulos, this restaurant is in a restored historic building by the sea, serving modern Greek dishes.
techne-hydra.com

OMILOS
Hydra
Suspended above the rocks, Omilos offers a privileged viewpoint of Hydra's port. Sit down to beef tartare, marinated sea bass and fresh pasta with ricotta in an elegant whitewashed setting.
omiloshydra.com

HYDRONETTA
Hydra
Hydra's most lively beach bar has steps that lead straight into the sea. Enjoy a refreshing dip followed by a cocktail and deep-fried feta parcels with honey and sesame (not the other way around).
Hydra 18040

SHOP

KOUTSIKOU
Hydra
A mother-and-daughter project, Koutsikou is a concept store with a selection of Italian and Greek brands of handmade ceramics, jewellery and clothing.
koutsikou.com

DO

DESTE
Hydra
An addition to the Deste Foundation in Athens, this outpost in Hydra hosts art exhibitions during the summer in the island's renovated former slaughterhouse, inviting visitors to unique site-specific shows.
deste.gr

KOUNDOURIOTIS HISTORICAL MANSION
Hydra
This historical home was at the centre of operations during the Greek War of Independence and was a site for political consultations following the revolution.
nhmuseum.gr

THE OLD CARPET FACTORY
Hydra
Overlooking the harbour of Hydra, the Old Carpet Factory was originally a workshop for rug weaving. Today it has turned into a music studio and artist residency, founded in 2015. Here musicians can escape modern distractions and embrace experimentation.
oldcarpetfactory.com

THESSALONIKI

Greece's second city is proud of its maritime roots and has a vibrant gastronomy scene. After periods under Byzantine, Ottoman and Venetian rule, Thessalonian society is a colourful mélange of communities, cultures and cuisines. Here's what should be at the top of your list.

STAY

ON RESIDENCE
Historic centre
On Residence has kept its belle époque essence, offering a journey through time with its neoclassical architecture, rich history and Olympos Naoussa restaurant.
onresidence.gr

THE MODERNIST
Historic centre
The Modernist is situated in downtown Thessaloniki and combines classical styles with Danish design. Ideal for travellers looking to settle in a laid back setting before hitting the town.
themodernisthotels.com

MONASTY
Historic centre
Moments from the city's porticoed Aristotelous Square, this discrete 100-key hotel opened in 2022 in a former Byzantine monastery. With the use of Persian samite silk in its interiors, Monasty pays homage to the precious textile that once clad the city's Byzantine emperors.
monastyhotel.com

MEDITERRANEAN PALACE
Historic centre
With a more ornate style and luxury atmosphere than other hotels in the area, the Mediterranean Palace offers views of the Thermaic Gulf and fine dining at Cookoo Restaurant.
mediterranean-palace.gr

EAT & DRINK

MOURGA
Historic centre
This pescatarian restaurant opened in 2017 and has been serving classic flavours and seasonal produce ever since. With a daily changing menu courtesy of chef and founder Ioannis Loukakis, Mourga offers fresh dishes based on catch and seasonality.
+30 23 1026 8826

Thessaloniki's White tower

SYNTROFÍ
Historic centre
A few blocks away from Aristotelous Square is Syntrofi, an open-kitchen restaurant serving dishes inspired by different Greek regions. The menu changes every day and offers a unique wine list.
Doxis 9

TIFFANY'S × 1905
Historic centre
On the site of another institution named Tiffany's that closed in 2013, the reimagined Tiffany's × 1905 now serves modern Greek cuisine in a crisp, light, minimalist setting.
tiffanys1905.gr

72H
Modiano market
An artisanal bakery located in the Modiano market stands out for its creative packaging and sourdough bread matured for 72 hours, hence the name. A blend of modernity and tradition comes through at 72H, a favourite for masterfully executed savoury and sweet baked goods.
agoramodiano.com

FATHER COFFEE & VINYL
Historic centre
Father Coffee & Vinyl is a spot in Thessaloniki where you can sip on a delicious daily blended coffee or one of the bar's signature cocktails while browsing the meticulous vinyl collection on sale.
Stratigou Kallari 9

YPSILON
Historic centre
Ypsilon is a café-cum-restaurant-cum-workspace in a beautiful 19th-century neoclassical building. A meeting place for the city's creative minds, this space hosts live music events and is pet friendly.
ypsilon.com.gr

STEREO
Historic centre
A hushed alternative to Thessaloniki's more boisterous night-time hangouts. Mingle with creative Thessalonians at the bistro tables that spill out into the street.
Dimarchou Vamvaka 3-5

ILIOPETRA
Ano Poli
One of Thessaloniki's most cherished restaurants serves Mediterranean fare with a view of the open kitchen, from which a steady stream of dishes of sardines in vine leaves, fresh tuna and fish roe emerge.
Eschilou 5

MAITR & MARGARITA
Historic centre
A hearty bistro with a focus on all things wine and craft beer. Try the bergamot orange risotto or braised pork cheeks, then wash it down with a pale ale brewed in-house.
maitrandmargarita.com

POSTER
Historic centre
The gastronomical arm of the Yiayia and Friends brand. Chef Vasilis Hamam creates a Greco-Levantine fusion. Expect *baba ganoush*, a *kyano* (blue cheese) dip and quince tarte tatin, washed down with an Arabic coffee.
posterrestaurant.gr

PELOSOF
Historic centre
Speciality coffee and Greek *tsoureki* pancakes with cinnamon cream and blueberries make for a hearty brunch at this open-plan industrial space. Come nightfall, you'll be lured in by the slick selection of cocktails and DJs.
Tsimiski 22

SHOP

ERGON AGORA EAST
Pilea Chortiatis
Bringing the food hall concept to Greece, Ergon combines a grocery store with a restaurant. The 6,000 sq m space also includes a beautiful outdoor garden, cinema and seaside bar.
ergonfoods.com

2ND FLOOR
Historic centre
Situated in a 1930s building at the heart of Thessaloniki, concept store 2nd floor displays international design and furniture pieces in an industrial setting, along with supplying interior design services.
2ndfloor.gr

YIAYIA AND FRIENDS
Historic centre
Known for their bright designs and packaging, olive oil brand Yiayia and Friends can be found in person at the store located in a historical building from 1905, offering healthy Greek snacks made from cereals and nuts as well as a range of premium-quality vinegars.
yiayiaandfriends.com

Museum of Byzantine Culture

PARA TODOS
Historic centre
Para Todos became a pioneer of elegant Greek men's fashion after it was founded in 2017. Inspired by the simplicity of Japanese attire and streetwear, Para Todos takes a cool and detailed approach to its designs.
paratodos.gr

KOTA THE STUDIO
Acheiropoietos
Three friends came together to found Kota in 2021. Here you'll find clay vases, wide-rimmed mugs and brightly coloured raki cups to adorn your kitchen counter.
Filippou 56

DO

STEREODISC
Historic centre
One of the oldest record shops in Greece, you will find exclusive prints at this beloved spot.
+30 23 1026 2912

POLYCENTRIC MUSEUM OF AIGAI
Vergina
Located on the borders of the city, the museum of the royal tombs is worth the short trip. The ruins that once constituted the capital of the Kingdom of Macedonia are one of the world's most impressive archaeological sites.
aigai.gr

MUSEUM OF PHOTOGRAPHY
Port of Thessaloniki
Promoting contemporary photography, the museum also carries an impressive collection of archives from renowned Greek photographers dating from the 19th century to present day.
momus.gr

MUSEUM OF BYZANTINE CULTURE
Saranta Ekklisies
A means of housing artefacts and artworks that honour the city's Byzantine heritage, Thessaloniki's Museum of Byzantine Culture was inaugurated in 1994. Inside are ancient coins, religious icons and ceramics dating from antiquity until the post-Byzantine period.
mbp.gr

THESSALONIKI WATERFRONT
Agia Triada
A public project intended to revitalise the city's seafront, the area now boasts a 3.5km-long area filled with public art and leisure facilities.
Thessaloniki 546 41

GREECE
The MONOCLE Handbook

ACKNOWLEDGEMENTS

MONOCLE

Editorial Director & Chairman
Tyler Brûlé

Editor in Chief
Andrew Tuck

Creative Director
Richard Spencer Powell

Production Director
Jacqueline Deacon

Chief Sub Editor
Lewis Huxley

Photography Director
Matthew Beaman

Art Director
Sam Brogan

MONOCLE BOOK OF GREECE

Head of Book Publishing
Virginia McLeod

Editor
Chiara Rimella

Deputy Editor
Amy van den Berg

Designer
Carey Alborough

Photography Editor
Sara Taglioretti

Sub Editor
Matt Dupuy

Writer
Claudia Jacob

Production Coordinator
Marta Fernàndez Canut

PRINCIPAL WRITERS

Amy van den Berg
Chiara Rimella
Claudia Jacob
Gabrielle Grangié
Katharine Sohn
Lucrezia Motta
Rory Jones

WRITERS

Anastasia Miari
Chloé Lake
Debbie Pappyn
Emilie Wade
Emmanuil Papavasileiou
Georgia Bisbas
Grace Charlton
Gunnar Gronlid
Hannah Lucinda Smith
Ilona Marx
Jack Simpson
Julia Lasica
Monica Lillis
Nathalie Savaricas
Nathalie Theodosi
Rachel Howard
Sonia Zhuravlyova
Stella Roos

RESEARCHERS

Conor McCann
Louis Harnett O'Meara
Mashal Butt
Tamsin Howard
Pádraig Belton

IMAGE LIBRARIES

Alamy
Anima Vision
Piraeus Bank Group Cultural
Foundation, N. Daniilidis
Shutterstock

ILLUSTRATORS

Nikolai Senin
Matteo Riva
Owen Gatley

PRINCIPAL PHOTOGRAPHERS

Louiza Vradi
Marco Arguello
Sarah Rainer
Thomas Gravanis

PHOTOGRAPHERS

Adrianna Glaviano
Alessandro Di Bon
Alex Kurunis
Alexandra Papoutsi
Alina Lefa
Alizée Gazeau
Ana Cuba
Andrea Pugiotto
Antonis Vlachos Dana Huertz
Benjamin Swanson
Chiara Goia
Chris Kontos
Claus Brechenmacher & Reiner
Baumann
David de Vleeschauwer
Ekaterina Juskowski
Filip Dujardin
Giorgos Sfakianakis
Ifigeneia Filopoulou
Ioanna Chatziandreou
James Mollison
Margarita Yoko Nikitaki
Marita Amorgianou
Mark Rammers
Mirto Iatropoulou
Nicholas Mastoris
Nonda Coutsicos
Panagiotis Voumvakis
Panos Davios
Paris Tavitian
Sophia Tolika
Sophie Knight
Stathis Mamalakis
Stefanos Tsakiris
Vassilis Karidis
Vasso Paraschi
Yannis Bournias
Yiorgos Kaplanidis
Yiorgos Kordakis
Yiorgos Mavropoulos

SPECIAL THANKS

Alexandra Aldeav
Anastasia Miari
Christina Martini
Daphne Karnezis
Emmanuil Papavasileiou
George Vamvakidis
John Papadimitriou
Lucy Kingett
Maria Lemos
Nathalie Savaricas
Nic Monisse
Vanessa Bird
Vangelis Liakos

Join our club

In 2007, MONOCLE was launched as a monthly magazine briefing on global affairs, business, design and more. Today we have a thriving print business, a radio station, shops, cafés, books, films and events. At our core is the simple belief that there will always be a place for a brand that is committed to telling fresh stories, delivering good journalism and being on the ground around the world. We're Zürich and London-based and have bureaux in Hong Kong, Paris, Tokyo and Toronto. Subscribe at *monocle.com*.

Monocle magazine

MONOCLE is published 10 times a year, including two double issues (July/August and December/January). We also have annual specials: THE FORECAST, THE ENTREPRENEURS and THE ESCAPIST. Look out for our seasonal newspapers too.

Monocle Radio

Our round-the-clock online radio station delivers global news and shows covering foreign affairs, urbanism, business, culture, food and drink, design and print media. You can listen live or download shows from *monocle.com/radio* – or wherever you get your podcasts.

Books

Since 2013, MONOCLE has been publishing books such as this one, covering a range of topics from home design to how to live a gentler life. Also available in this series are Handbooks for Portugal, Spain and France. All our books are available on our website, through our distributor, Thames & Hudson, or at all good bookshops.

Monocle Minute

MONOCLE's smartly appointed family of newsletters comes from our team of editors and bureau chiefs around the world. From the daily *Monocle Minute* to *The Monocle Weekend Editions* and our weekly *Monocle On Design* special, sign up to get the latest in affairs, entrepreneurship and design, straight to your inbox every day – all for free. Sign up at *monocle.com/minute*.

MONOCLE